SCREAMS OF THE DROWNING

SCREAMS OF THE DROWNING

DROWNING

From the Eastern Front to the Sinking of the *Gustloff*

Klaus Willmann

(As told to him by Hans Fackler)

Foreword by
Roger Moorhouse

Translated by
Eva Burke

Greenhill Books

Screams of the Drowning
This English-language edition
first published in 2021 by
Greenhill Books,
c/o Pen & Sword Books Ltd,
47 Church Street, Barnsley,
S. Yorkshire, S70 2AS

www.greenhillbooks.com
contact@greenhillbooks.com

ISBN: 978–1–78438–598–9

Publishing History
First published in German in 2019 as
Schreie der Ertrinkenden
by Edition Förg (Rosenheim).
This is the first English-language edition
and includes a new foreword by Roger Moorhouse.

CIP data records for this title are available from the British Library

Designed and typeset by Donald Sommerville

Printed and bound in the UK by TJ Books Ltd, Padstow

Typeset in 11.5/15 pt Minion Pro

Contents

Translator's Note

It was a delicate task to translate *Screams of the Drowning*, written in the first person and as the personal memoir of Hans Fackler, a Wehrmacht soldier who survived the sinking of the *Wilhelm Gustloff*. While Hans is the protagonist, the journalist Klaus Willmann, who interviewed Hans, becomes the chronicler.

From this perspective it is a memoir once removed, but very much allows Hans's own voice to resonate as principal narrator. Complicating the matter slightly further, Hans himself speaks in two registers: as a young lad enlisted in Germany's Wehrmacht who fought in Russia, and as an elderly gentleman interviewed late in his life, who has the advantage of hindsight and reflection. Willmann, the author, known to be an honest and meticulous journalist with an acute ear, was mindful to keep the registers apart, fluidly moving between the two via the narrative device of a stream of consciousness from which he could break out by inserting helpful signposts such as 'thinking back' or 'now that I know', thereby allowing for authenticity. But within the stream of consciousness, the close reader might be left wondering. Were those really, genuinely the true thoughts of the protagonist at the time? Of his comrades?

Roughly the book is divided as follows: Hans Fackler's early years of training; the gruesome realities of Hitler's war during its final years; the horrendous experience of being on the sinking *Wilhelm Gustloff*; and Hans building his civilian life in post-war Germany.

Hans had not received higher education, just like so many of his fellow recruits who were either too young or not from the privileged classes. His language in the first section remains simple and straightforward, but is nevertheless colourful and vivid, often offering us idioms commonly used by young men in Germany of that time and rarely encountered today.

The language of killing as a sport or game is reiterated in the vocabulary of killing to inflict death in section two.

The climax of the book is the sinking of the *Wilhelm Gustloff*. I feel that *Untergang*, the German word for 'sinking', more accurately describes the cruise-liner-turned-military transport's final journey into the depths of the sea and is mirrored in the *Untergang* of the Third Reich covered in the last chapters. *Untergang* more harshly connotes loss, ruin, doom, death and destruction and allows us to linguistically put side by side the visual worlds conjured up in the collective memory of *Gustloff* survivors and of Germans suffering the demise of what was once the German Reich. Hans identifies with both. The screams of the drowning are echoed in the screams of Hans's compatriots struggling in a ruined post-war Germany whose economy is in tatters.

For the sake of clarity, I have referred to towns and cities by their official names in their country before 1945, with notes to confirm their modern identities. That is not to imply any ongoing German claim to any of the cities but rather to avoid confusion, because the German sources rarely used Polish, Czech, or other languages' names for towns and cities under their occupation. For German cities, I have maintained German spelling unless the city is particularly well known by its English equivalent (hence Pocking or Garmisch, but Nuremberg, rather than Nürnberg, and Munich rather than München).

Military ranks are usually translated from German to their nearest equivalent English titles. Some German ranks were created specifically for the Reich Labour Service (RAD) or the SS or the Nazi Party itself and no longer exist, and in those cases the ranks are retained in their German originals.

In the same vein, I have preserved some words, terms, concepts and slogans widely used by the Nazi regime, having been either coined by Adolf Hitler himself and other Nazi Party members or borrowed from everyday German in order to redefine a perverted reality; and some songs referred to in the book were previously existing popular German songs appropriated by the Nazi regime with some changes to the lyrics.

To give a flavour of German wartime history, some specific terms used by or about soldiers have been retained in German, such as Landser, the everyday word for an ordinary soldier, roughly equivalent to the British 'Tommy' of the American 'GI'.

Eva Burke

Foreword

Life can come at you fast, sometimes. Never more so, perhaps, than for the generation of Germans born in the mid-1920s. For them, coming to adolescence with the outbreak of war in 1939, they were plunged headlong into a world for which they were scarcely prepared, driven by a regime whose horrors they could scarcely yet comprehend.

Hans Fackler was a member of that generation. Born in 1926, he grew up in Munich, in a world where Nazi ideology wasn't questioned, where service 'to *Führer* and Fatherland' was a given. His war, when it came, progressed like that of so many other ordinary Germans of his age: the enthusiastic call-up, the mind-numbing training, and the camaraderie, forged in adversity. His national service began with an obligatory stint in the RAD (*Reichsarbeitsdienst*) labour service, before joining his unit just past his seventeenth birthday – the end of what he calls his 'curtailed youth'. He first saw action in modern-day Ukraine, the following spring, participating in what had, by then, become a long, bloody retreat by German forces. The enemy were most often unseen; a silhouette, a flash of earth-brown uniform, a terrifying chorus of 'Urrah!' from advancing soldiers. Yet they were ubiquitous. Death was ever-present; so much so that the young Fackler quickly grew numb to it, immune to its horrors. 'It no longer mattered', he wrote, 'whether it was them or us.'

In time, however, he would come to see quite enough of the Red Army. Selected for a special operation, he would form the fighting tail of his unit's retreat, blowing up bridges, destroying stores – anything that would slow the Soviet advance and aid his comrades' escape. Much of his account is highly illustrative of the problems that the German Army faced in the last years of the war: no air cover, not enough armour, too little fuel and too many lice. Ordinary soldiers such as Fackler fought bravely and with considerable ingenuity, but they couldn't withstand a Soviet juggernaut that was more mobile, better equipped and better fed. Injured by shrapnel in the defence of Königsberg, he was finally earmarked for evacuation home.

Ordinarily, one might imagine that this would be the end of the story: his injury prefacing a spell in a field hospital, a perilous trudge west and a long recuperation amid the ruins of the once all-conquering Reich. But it is here that Fackler's story takes its most fascinating turn, as he is slated to be carried west, via the Baltic Sea, aboard the MV *Wilhelm Gustloff*, thereby making him an unwitting participant in one of the most gruesome episodes of the European war.

The story of the *Wilhelm Gustloff* is growing in recognition, but is still under-known, considering its magnitude. For those unaware, the *Gustloff* was a purpose-built cruise liner, commissioned by Hitler's government for the use of the KdF, the entertainment arm of the German Workers Front – the Nazi 'trade union'. Vessels like the *Gustloff* spearheaded the Nazi seduction of the German populace; offering subsidised cruises to Norway, Portugal or the Mediterranean, as tangible, irrefutable proof of the 'benefits' of Nazi rule.

By January 1945, however, the *Gustloff* had been mothballed, having spent the war first as a hospital ship, then as a floating barracks, moored in the harbour at Gdynia – which the Germans renamed Gotenhafen – home to a flotilla of U-Boat cadets. In the gathering maelstrom of the final months of the war, she would be brought out of retirement, and – like countless other German merchant vessels – press-ganged into service to aid the escape of countless thousands of civilians and injured soldiers from the Eastern Front. The operation of which the *Gustloff* was a part – Operation Hannibal – is similarly obscure, yet it remains the largest seaborne evacuation in history, bringing over a million people to the safety of Kiel, Stralsund or Swinemünde. In that effort, some ships would make numerous crossings, repeatedly braving the freezing waters of the Baltic, where Soviet submarines lurked unseen. The *Gustloff* would make only one.

Hans Fackler boarded the *Wilhelm Gustloff* at the end of January 1945 in Gdynia. His account of the episode is necessarily rather vague, given that he was heavily sedated at the time, but it is likely that he was taken from Pillau (now Baltysk) to Gdynia aboard the cargo ship *Reval*, and loaded onto the *Gustloff* just prior to its departure from Gdynia on the afternoon of 30 January. That same night, the *Gustloff* was off the coast of Pomerania when, as Fackler describes, she was hit by three torpedoes – fired by the Soviet submarine *S-13* – and sank within a little under an hour. Fackler's escape from the vessel is remarkable, not only because he was stretcher-bound and there were few functioning lifeboats – but also because of the sheer crush of desperate humanity that he left behind him. He was one of only 1,252 people who survived the catastrophe. Over 9,000 did not. The sinking of the *Wilhelm Gustloff* is the worst maritime disaster in history.

Ordinarily, an event of such drama and horror as this would warrant boundless popular interest, spawning numerous books, films and documentaries. Yet, until comparatively recently, the sinking of the *Wilhelm Gustloff* was little-known; the niche preserve of a few obsessive specialists and a dwindling band of survivors. Seen in that light, one can appreciate the historical significance of this book; there are comparatively few accounts of the sinking itself. And, though Fackler's story of the grim fate of the *Gustloff* occupies only a small proportion of the book, it is nonetheless new, and is the stunning, cataclysmic denouement to his narrative, a memory 'forever engraved' in his mind. It is that which, to a large extent, sets his story apart.

For those readers immune to such arcane concerns, this book can be read simply as an engaging, well-written account of a young man thrust into the must murderous theatre of the most murderous war in human history. His view is necessarily narrow, restricted by his age and his lowly status, but it is searing nonetheless. When he left for the Eastern Front in 1943, Fackler can scarcely have imagined what the next two years would have in store for him. His story is a reminder that life can always spring a surprise, and fate can be a capricious mistress.

Roger Moorhouse

Preface

Several years ago I was alerted to an article that appeared in the *Süddeutsche Zeitung* and the *Münchner Merkur* focusing on a Hans Fackler, originally from the Ebersberg county in Upper Bavaria. The brief article led me to visit Herr Fackler, a man well into his nineties who was happy for me to write his story. In our meetings Hans described his experiences from the time when he was a young soldier and through the difficult war years, all of which I recount in this narrative as truthfully as I am able to.

His story aims to be everything except a glorification of heroic war acts. In fact, he wants to make it patently obvious to the younger generation that peace is never anything but the period between wars. He feels, therefore, that the fact that we citizens of West and Middle Europe won't end up banging our heads against each other is not something we can take for granted these days.

Indeed, ever since 8 May 1945, and after some considerable difficulties in the earlier days, we – and I am referring primarily to our country as well as those with which we are united as allies – have been able to enjoy peace for over seventy-five years, a time span encompassing more than two generations. This fact, in my opinion, must not tempt any of our young politicians who have not themselves experienced the horrors of war to consider peace as a given.

Quite the contrary: peace is fragile, and any poorly conceived act, even so much as an ill-chosen word or a comment dropped casually in conversation could destabilise this precious equilibrium and derail all efforts to sustain it.

All we can wish and hope for is that a peaceful Europe might live on, that we continue to thrive in our communities and avoid armed conflict in which, as we know full well, it is mostly the civilian community that ends up suffering. Wherever war rages today, it behoves us to do all we can to bring about peace.

Klaus Willmann

Bellmann

Biloxi

Miss

Schleswig

Gorman

CHAPTER 1

My Childhood and Curtailed Youth

Shortly before I was born, my father died in a car accident in the vicinity of Berlin. I therefore grew up in a one-parent family. Subsequently my mother and I moved to a rented flat in Munich and I started school, with teachers still very much in a mindset overshadowed by the defeat we had suffered in the First World War. For many people the uppermost goal was to do all they could to foster the nationalism that had survived the Imperial era and had filtered into the Weimar Republic – all in the face of what they perceived to be the disgraceful position that the Versailles Peace Treaty had relegated them to.

Day in and day out they seemed to be struggling with this shame, and our class teacher was no different. It had its advantages in that he oftentimes kept us spellbound with the fascinating adventures he had experienced during his career as an officer on the Western Front. The story which captivated me most was when he described his imprisonment by the French, when he and his comrades were in a camp outside a burned-down factory. Though the jailers had put them under strict surveillance, they had managed, thus ran the tale, to dig a tunnel underneath the fence, all the while ingeniously hiding the excavated earth. They were never found out and their escape was successful. 'I took fifteen men with me and we got away undetected', he would brag. 'It was a brilliant escape route and above all allowed us to rejoin our troops.'

More often than not he would conclude his narrative with an ominous prediction of the future: 'I am quite sure that all of you youngsters will end up seeing a new war.' He spoke, of course, at a time when Hitler and the NSDAP were already in government, and there was hardly anybody who could ignore the extraordinary lengths to which the regime went in order to restore the German Army and militarise the people. The enormous propaganda machine they deployed to reach this goal was quite staggering.

Us lads didn't really take any of these prophecies seriously. As far as we were concerned, war simply seemed to be nothing else than one big and exciting adventure. So, we continued to enjoy our freedom outside school hours and relished serving in the Jungvolk – the section of the Hitler Youth [Hitler Jugend – HJ] which ten to fourteen-year-old German boys were initially encouraged by the state to join, but which later became compulsory. Naturally, being young, we were very much attracted by the uniform of brown shirts and short black trousers, but it was above all the black belt from which dangled a hunting knife that really took our fancy. It was a period in history in which German society was characterised by who wore which uniform.

Born in 1926, I along with all those comrades born in that year, naturally progressed to the Hitler Youth the moment I celebrated my fourteenth birthday, and straight after graduating from my junior school. This was the only youth organisation permitted and promoted by the Nazis, and became obligatory in 1939. Truth be told, none of us felt that being a member was in any way burdensome; in fact it was quite the contrary. The sense of belonging, the whiff of adventure experienced during our excursions, the taste of camaraderie around the blazing camp fires, the cross-country games and other paramilitary events – all this filled us with pure joy. Throughout my apprenticeship as a joiner from the time when I was merely fourteen years old, I enthusiastically embraced all activities offered in the Hitler Youth. As for the ideological indoctrination which was part and parcel of the movement, it didn't even enter into my mind to question it in any way; it was a given.

During the first years of the war we lived in an apartment block located at Robert Koch Strasse 14, with a tiny convenience store around the corner where my mother used to buy our milk, eggs and other groceries. At that time, food was already being rationed, and ever-hungry lads like myself were seldom full. I still remember quite vividly how mother once returned home with an empty shopping bag and was clearly annoyed. 'I honestly couldn't restrain myself today,' she blustered, 'when all the shelves in the store stared back at me totally empty, I just lost my temper. There wasn't even a morsel of bread to be had. Well,' she continued in full swing, 'didn't I give them a piece of my mind . . . Hitler can kiss my arse, is what I told them . . . didn't I, why, he can't even provide for his own people!'

The following day, a Sunday, we were sitting at our kitchen table with a sparse breakfast set before us, when the bell rang at our front door. I opened it and saw two middle-aged men standing opposite me, both wearing broad-brimmed hats and grey coats. The older one eyed me up with a stern look on his face, but I noticed some surprise in his eyes. As I was heading out to join a Hitler Youth meeting due to start in the next half hour at the Alter Hof, I was already dressed in my brown shirt and black shorts – precisely according to regulations.

'Is your mother at home?' The other man asked me.

'Yes, why?'

'Why don't we tell her ourselves,' he said brusquely and pushed past me before I could even step to the side. Suddenly, there they were standing in the middle of our small kitchen severely scrutinising my mother, their manner ominous. 'Frau Fackler,' the older one spoke, his tone threatening, 'what were you thinking, I ask you, when you went shopping and decided yesterday to insult our Führer so publicly?'

I could only marvel at my mother's intrepid response. 'What's that you're saying?' she faced them square in the face and put on quite an indignant manner. 'Shopping, you say? This was supposed to have happened while I was out shopping? I can assure you, *meine Herren*, this is one hell of an exaggeration, as once again, there was precious little I was able to buy! I am sorry that this slipped out of my mouth . . . but I was just so angry . . . This has absolutely nothing to do with my views, if that is what it's all about! You are welcome to ask anybody in the building and make your enquiries about me, should you still have any doubts.'

'We've already covered this, Frau Fackler, we know what we're about, seeing as we're from the Gestapo, and you can thank your lucky stars that all reports about you have turned out in your favour. But we must nevertheless issue you with a strict warning. Should we happen to get wind of even the tiniest criticism raised against you, you will definitely not get off as lightly as this time round!' Both men stood to attention, whipped out their right arms, extended them straight out and shouted in unison: '*Heil Hitler!*' Spontaneously I too clicked my heels together and imitated the salute, noting from the corner of my eye that my mother also had her arm raised for the Hitler salute, but meanwhile the two men had already made their way out of the flat.

This wasn't the only surprise of that day. Later on, just when my pal Gerhard Hugel and I, along with another comrade from our HJ corps were about to enter the hall, we had to pass a very pretty young lady dressed in a blue uniform. She was sitting at a small table taking down the names, dates of birth and addresses of every one of us. Looking at each other slightly startled, but not even able to utter a word, we could already see a young lieutenant – proudly wearing the Iron Cross emblem on his shirt – approaching us. 'How would you like to become a member of the *Hermann Göring* Division?' he asked in a friendly enough manner, adding 'I've already convinced some of your comrades to sign up.'

The other guy who had arrived with me and Gerhard could barely contain his excitement and loudly responded 'Yes, lieutenant, I too report as a volunteer and want to join this elite division,' he saluted with his face flushed with self-satisfaction.

'Thank you!' replied the lieutenant, 'Congratulations. I applaud your decision.'

Turning to Gerhard and me he repeated his question and my friend took a step forward, thanked the lieutenant for the offer and politely added: 'I will, with permission, think about this a little bit.'

'Of course, you may give this more thought! But, quite honestly, I'm puzzled as to what it might be that a healthy German youngster wants to mull over.' He then looked at me quizzically and, feeling rather pressured, I felt it best to agree on the spot, letting him know in a firm tone that I would, of course, join my buddy and sign up.

With a friendly hand gesture, the recruiter then waved for me to follow the others, who had meanwhile already gathered in the hall that was filling up with lively chatter.

Thus it was, in the summer of 1942, when I was sixteen, it was my turn to be dispatched to one of the many Wehrmacht training camps at the Hohenkammer Schloss in Upper Bavaria. As far as I was concerned, it was a welcome change from the tedious routine of my life at home, on top of which it carried the added bonus of staying at a historic castle nestled within the picturesque and serene countryside north-west of Munich. This was my first experience undergoing military drill, with its unconditional obedience, its harsh physical training and relentless instruction in the use of firearms.

In those middle years of the war, our successes and victories filled us with unimaginable enthusiasm. Our German Wehrmacht seemed to be invincible, with the radio continuously broadcasting special reports on our achievements.

Curiously, what mattered above all to our camp leader was the absolute necessity for us to all march in one straight line. Secondly, our singing had to be loud. 'Sure, the march should be tuneful, naturally, but make damn sure that you can be heard far and wide,' is what they continuously drilled into us, and so we would literally be screaming out the words of all the different military and propaganda songs, like. 'Trembling are the rotten bones':

> Trembling are the rotten bones
> Of the world before the Red War.
> We smashed the terror,
> For us it was a great victory.
>
> We will march on
> Even when everything falls in shards,
> For today Germany listens to us
> And tomorrow the whole world.[*]

---

[*] Hans Baumann's *Es zittern die morschen Knochen* ('Trembling are the rotten bones') became the official marching song of the Reich Labour Service. The line 'Germany listens to us' in the original composition was also usually later reworded as 'Germany belongs to us'.

Not one of us would have guessed that what these songs were actually meant to achieve was for us to become inspired and powerful fighters. Ideology was key, and all of us had been made well aware that no one should dare question or hesitate over joining the armed forces promptly. Those in charge were adamant about licking us into shape with only one goal in mind: to pile victories on top of those already achieved.

But there were three lads amongst the hundred soldiers in our camp who immediately attracted attention. Whether this was due to their blatant lack of interest or their reclusive behaviour, we never found out. I am equally not quite sure whether what ensued was because our educators condoned an established tradition or whether indeed it was an idea my comrades had come up with; regardless, within just two days the three guys had their heads totally shaved, and were then tied up in a cloth sack and sorely beaten.

On my return home my mother showed me a newspaper article which reported on life in the camp and had a picture of us marching in one straight column, with me clearly visible in the front row, as that is where I had been placed due to my unusual height. Obviously proud, she had kept the clipping, which must have got lost or burnt later on, along with so many other papers, as a result of the air raids which had razed my hometown.

Immediately after I had completed my apprenticeship exams at the age of seventeen, I got the call-up letter requesting me to present myself for the physical examination at the Hofbräukeller. My mother and I certainly couldn't afford to frequent any pubs in Munich, and so I had no idea where any of them were located. So, after some discussion, I reported to the Hofbräuhaus, much to the amusement of the staff there. 'What, sonny, you say that you're a local and are confusing the Hofbräuhaus with the Hofbräukeller?'

A tall, slim waiter, already greying at the temples, had in the meantime approached me and looked me up and down, 'What we have here is beer,' he muttered, not being able to hide his disdain, 'there's no recruiting around here, good fellow, now do us a favour and get lost.' Embarrassed, I took my leave. How was I to know? Until that day I had been extremely busy with my apprenticeship, with the HJ and attending the *Heimabende** or, if I had some free time, I spent it kicking a ball around on the football pitch. The inside of a bar was definitely a novelty for the likes of me. But I was annoyed, nonetheless, that somebody could feel free just to have a go at me.

Half an hour later I was standing in a long queue, and after a long wait I came face to face with a doctor who performed a rather superficial health check on us. It came as no surprise to me that I was put into the *kv*† category as I was completely healthy, as fit as a fiddle, which was not least because I had never been mollycoddled.

Not a week had passed when I got my call-up note for the Reich Labour Service [RAD] ordering me to report to the barracks in Zellmühleck. That small hamlet was situated in the Bavarian Oberland, close to the Alps and in the midst of a forest not far from the Kochelsee, and even today it doesn't consist of much more than a clutch of a few farms. When the weather was fine we would enjoy a view reaching from the top of the Herzogstand and the Heimgarten – we could even make out the huge water pipes leading down from the Walchensee, located above – down to the electricity works that had been installed at the shore of the Kochelsee. The barracks were subdivided into rooms to each of which twelve men had been allocated. We were assigned very simple double bunks made out of spruce: three beds were located along the right side and three on the left side, leaving only a very narrow space in the middle which reached from the entrance at one end to the window on the other end, and was so tight you could hardly move around. In between the bunk beds were our lockers. While we were busying ourselves with placing our belongings in these lockers, the unit leader interrupted our chatter and made it quite clear that in the camp the tone used to communicate with each other was to be of a short military nature; it had to be to the point, even rough.

---

* *Heimabende* – 'evenings at home'. These were in fact evenings spent at HJ clubhouses writing letters to soldiers or wrapping parcels for the front and participating in programmes meant to instil ideology and enthusiasm for the war.

† kv = *kriegsverwendungsfähig* = 'fit for war service'.

One of the guys I shared the room with and who had been on my train journey was Fritz Berger, who hailed from Munich and who would become a good friend of mine during our time in the service. Once, in the midst of one of those especially tough dressing downs by our superior, he tried to calm me down. 'Hans,' he whispered for only me to hear. 'Just ignore that show-off, let him scream his head off and don't worry . . . we'll definitely put these six months of RAD behind us, no problem.'

Our superiors, the Feldmeister for one, were offered lodgings in a much more comfortable barrack block situated on a slight rise, which thus allowed them not only to look down on us lot, but also afforded them a splendid view over the hilly Alps. There was no jealousy on my part, however, as I knew that these guys had to make this place their home and remain here much longer than we did.

The subsequent months of what was left of our summer were filled with being ordered to build roads through the forest, enlarge a bridge over a river, all while being trained in a whole slew of regular army jobs. The part I despised most was the rifle drill in which we had to use our polished spades in lieu of the real thing. Curiously it wasn't even the higher-ranking superiors who proved the worst bullies, but the team leaders. 'If after your six months spent here with us you actually manage to move on to regular army barracks, we sure don't want any poor performance on your part to reflect on us! We won't stand for a bad reputation or be accused that we have failed as educators just because of you sad bunch of losers! So let's see it, you lazy bones, get a grip on yourselves! What do you think we're doing . . . running a nursery?' Just about daily would such insults be hurled across the gravelled courtyard, which by then we had all grown to hate with a passion.

There were no bathrooms for us so we had to wash ourselves out in the open with only cold water dribbling out of a water spout from a protruding iron pipe fixed above a stone trough, just as we find them today outside mountain huts for cattle to drink from. Regardless, we had to appear spotless, and those who in the eyes of our superiors didn't cut the mustard lived to regret it. Not only did they have to endure bitter insults, but oftentimes were physically abused or penalised and forced, for example, to complete hundreds of excruciating knee bends, push-ups, or perform endless bunny hops with arms outstretched. It seemed that these petty tyrants had an inexhaustible imagination when it came to sanctions. As for us, how much we commiserated with the poor chap who had been picked upon was probably commensurate with how much we liked him.

During my stint at the RAD we experienced around three air raids which, though none of us dared say it out loud, rather dimmed our faith in victory, that had until then been steadfast and unswerving. Had anyone even uttered the slightest concern, he would have been severely reprimanded, as it would have been tantamount to subversion, undermining military morale, and would have invariably entailed a torturous punishment.

During the first of these nights we were standing in front of our barracks and could see how the city beneath us glowed in the light of the firebombs. The family of Heinz Strauch, my comrade, lived in Solln, a district in Munich. Standing next to me he got terribly incensed. 'So here they are, our supposed clueless enemy, managing to unload their heavy stuff undisturbed,' he fumed. 'What the hell is going on with our Luftwaffe, has it really become so weak?' he asked, without expecting anyone to give him a satisfactory answer. 'What has happened to those famous words our fat Air Marshal Göring proclaimed: "If even a single enemy airplane crosses our Reich, feel free to call me Meier." I won't even mention other cities like Hamburg or Cologne,' he continued. 'What's taking place here is atrocious!' he raged. 'This Herr Obermeier of ours should be embarrassed.'

'Heinz!' exclaimed another mate. 'I'm going to pretend not to have heard what you've just said.' Continuing in the same chastising tone, he added: 'May I give you my two pennies worth: you've gotten far too used to thinking out loud and,' at this point his voice sounded more threatening, 'if you foolishly loosen your tongue even more, you may well find yourself working somewhere else much sooner than you think – in a KZ for example.'* Heinz just mumbled something inaudible.

---

* KZ, pronounced as *Ka-Zet*. = *Konzentrationslager* – concentration camp.

The following day we were sent to help clear up the mess in Munich.

Together with some of my comrades, we started off by removing the mounds of shards that were heaped up in front of the villa of our RAD leader, then moved on to replacing shattered windows, broken window panes, and refurbished the loft which had all but completely collapsed, filling in the gaping holes in the roof with proper tiles. It goes without saying that we had, of course, representatives of just about every construction category on our team. Once finished, we were detailed to other prestigious villas in Grünwald, the most exclusive area of the city.

Heinz Strauch, working alongside me, couldn't help himself but continue making comments, ignoring the unequivocal hint our comrade had dropped before. 'Hans,' he muttered without turning towards me, 'only party bigwigs live here, they must have bombed this place on purpose . . . But, wouldn't you know it,' he pointed out sarcastically, 'we've got just about everything we need to fix whatever is even slightly damaged, every single material you could wish for in just about the best quality – that's what has been made available here. And yesterday,' he had worked himself into quite a state 'just yesterday both of us could see with our own eyes that other than a few of the HJ boys, pretty much nobody could care less about the damage caused and the debris that surrounds us all as well as the rest of the city. People simply have to get on with things, fix the mess by themselves and be grateful for any planks of wood they can put their hands on, or some nails to board up the windows . . . And look at the handsome supply we've got here . . . There sure seems to be enough glass to be had!'

'For God's sake, Heinz, stop thinking out loud,' I whispered back. 'For one thing, nothing has happened to our families.'

'And that's just because they were damn lucky,' Heinz retorted softly.

We were kept busy in Grünwald from Monday to Saturday, slept in a gym hall on a bed of straw, and received much better food than back at the camp. During the following months we were called in twice more to carry out such clear-up operations around the city.

In autumn 1943 an American fighter plane was shot down and plummeted into the Kochelsee, scattering debris across its steep wooded banks. Nobody could quite pinpoint exactly where it had crashed, but for us it was a welcome distraction from the monotonous RAD routine, and we quite enjoyed spending two days (unsuccessfully) trying to locate the pilot.

At the end of each of these days searching from morning to evening and the moment we returned to base, we had to go through with a uniform inspection. We were fully aware of the power our superiors wielded over us and how scrupulously they adhered to the smallest detail of the rule book. They would scrutinise the tiniest part of our equipment, check our underwear and inspect our uniform for the most minor faults. This invariably caused some of my comrades sleepless nights, with them getting deeply upset when their boots, for example, were found not polished well enough, or when their lockers had supposedly not been stacked according to the rule book, or if any other trivial inaccuracy was pointed out. Meanwhile I could speak of good fortune, as never once was I accosted by one of the corporals who would gleefully lash out at the culprits and chase them across the courtyard of the barracks screaming and yelling at them and showering them with curses and the wildest insults.

Yet there was one aspect of our RAD days which I, along with three other comrades of my unit of some forty men, very much enjoyed. The four of us were joiner apprentices and thus, of course, we were all rather talented at woodwork. This would see us, after training and once we had accomplished all our duties, gathering around to craft small boats, cribs, cars and other such toys in aid of the Winter Relief Fund. Allegedly these items were to be given to needy children whose fathers had been separated from their families due to having been drafted to the army.

Incidentally, and coming back to the American pilot for whom we had been searching, we would only find out quite some time later that his body had been found and salvaged from the Kochelsee, but by that time I was already serving as a young recruit with the pioneers in Ingolstadt.

CHAPTER 2

Training and First Experiences

Because of my height I was usually ordered to march alongside two other tall comrades in the front row of our column. Truth be told, we weren't necessarily a beautiful sight to behold, but our loud singing voices filling the air on our way from the barracks across the city square to our training positions certainly impressed everyone we passed. Those smaller than us and therefore placed in the rear kept urging us not to take such large steps, as they'd get out of breath, weren't able to sing and couldn't keep up, or so they claimed. 'Not everyone's got legs as long as you three!' they moaned.

Their pleas came to us in a whisper as our strict overseers weren't meant to catch wind of their complaints. Having been given a taste of the so-called *Sonderbehandlung** during our very first few days at the barracks, we knew what would be in store for us if we spoke out of turn or, indeed, did anything however minor it might seem in our eyes that was considered contrary to the rule book by those in charge.

Our barracks were situated close to the Danube, and the days we spent training there seemed endless, although there were relatively few of them. We were instructed in how to link two riverbanks in record time by using so-called pontoons – buoyant floats made of solid steel which connected bridge sections to each other, allowing even very heavy vehicles to cross. While toiling away on a bridge, I would often find real pride surging within me. We Germans, we certainly had the engineering skills covered and what we achieved proved it, I thought proudly.

---

* *Sonderbehandlung* – Special Treatment – a euphemism for rough handling, torture and murder under the Nazis.

Speaking of feeling proud and confident – thinking back, I am not sure whether or not it was a coincidence, but it was a fact that the majority of our recruits had learned a trade. We knew our crafts and were a skilful and hardened lot. Actually, I sometimes pitied the few mummies'-boys amongst our group when they became the butt of our instructors' quite relentless ridicule – mostly it was the corporals who were the guilty party, but sergeants would also join in this sort of public humiliation and ruthless mockery. Some of our comrades were also to blame, though all they did was stand and observe from the sideline.

Regardless, the paramilitary training that we had previously completed with the HJ had certainly left a noticeable and positive impact on most of us. Here, as in the past, the motto prevailed: 'Agile as a greyhound, tough as leather, hard as Krupp steel.'* No German youngster, and certainly no man, was to be found crying. Not one of us was consciously aware that we had, in fact, been trained to function like military robots. And this was not new. 'The rifle is the soldier's bride!' was a saying that was drilled into us at all times and everywhere, not only on the range. 'Mind our warning and treat her properly, one day your life may depend on handling her deftly!'

I was quite aware that ever since my training at the barracks I had been a decent shot, but when, one day, I was singled out for having scored the highest number of hits after our first live fire practice I was still taken by surprise. It didn't take long before I had the reputation of being the most competent marksman in my company, which of course earned me a good standing with my superiors, but never went to my head. I made sure of that. Once, thanks to my especially noteworthy shooting scores at a particular event, I was rewarded with a day off, which I thoroughly enjoyed, and as far as I was concerned this was enough of an acknowledgement for someone like me.

Hardly anyone will dispute the historic truth that since antiquity humankind has devoted time and resources to advancing the

---

* *'Flink wie die Windhunde, zäh wie Leder, hart wie Kruppstahl'*. Krupp was Germany's leading iron and steel maker, using many thousands of save labourers under the Nazis.

development of instruments of war. It was no different in our times and thus we were instructed in how to lay mines, how to deactivate them and how to deal with anti-tank weapons. We young lads were of the firm belief that we would win this war or, at the very least, weren't allowed to lose it. Each one of us, as far as I could tell, put our heart and soul into that war.

Towards the end of November 1943 my group, all dressed in combat uniform and accompanied by the sounds of a brass band, were marched off to the train station. There, we were ordered to board a freight train where we also stowed all of our technical equipment. The destination was as yet unknown to us, but when we reached Salzburg, rumours circulated that we were headed for Yugoslavia. 'The people in that country have been at each other's throats for generations,' we were told. 'But now they've discovered that they have us Germans as their common enemy, their leader, this chap Tito, has gone and united them against us! They've become cheeky, these folk . . . and only God knows what'll be awaiting us there.'

Dark thoughts began to trouble me. Was a partisan war looming? Such a war would not have any defined front lines, that much I knew. Nobody would know where the enemy lay in ambush and from where the bullets might be fired. We'd surely have our work cut out!

But I certainly didn't dare voice my concerns out loud and gradually the carefree nonchalance of youth prevailed. 'Hans,' I said to myself: 'nothing will happen to you, you can rely on that!' And so I continued having a good laugh with my comrades on that platform while eyeing up one or two pretty young Red Cross nurses standing around in their neat uniforms, as young and excited as us. The tea handed out by some helpful Salzburg matrons wasn't particularly tasty, and one of the young ladies noticed our grimaces. Approaching me with a cheeky grin, she stood up close, and swiftly pulling a flat flask out of her pocket she surreptitiously poured a shot of rum into my cup. 'Might this taste better now?' she asked with a mischievous twinkle in her bright-blue eyes.

While our lot largely mainly originated from the southern parts of Germany, there were also some lads from Berlin among us, and some from the Rhineland and East Prussia. There were even a few from the Sudetenland. But this in no way spoiled the sense of camaraderie.

After just an hour or so, our rather pleasant stay in Salzburg came to an abrupt end. 'All aboard!'

While our long freight train slowly rolled out of the Salzburg station, I leaned far out of the wagon door and tried to wave to my merry female beneficiary. Then, drawing in my neck for a brief second, I lost sight of the white cloth she had been waving above her head.

When the train came to a stop during the night in a siding at a station in Croatia, a sprightly youngster from Hamburg turned to me. 'They sure don't seem to be in a hurry to get us wherever it is they want us to go,' he observed. In that moment a train loaded with tanks whooshed past us. Hörmann, our rascal from Vienna, quickly identified its destination. 'Boys,' he declared, 'That train is definitely headed for Greece, not Yugoslavia!'

'And how, pray tell,' responded a baritone voice in a clearly detectable Swabian accent, 'might you be able to be so cock-sure?'

'I know the train driver from the other train, Lieutenant Zwerger,' he replied, unfazed. 'He's from St Pölten and told me back in Salzburg that at one point on our journey we would be overtaken by a freight train carrying tanks. It was, he assured me, confirmed in his schedule.'

'Pity, that!' someone else butted in, 'We could use a few of these tanks against that Tito fellow!'

'Pah, don't you worry, good chap,' yet another know-it-all chimed in, 'we'll clean up that dope in no time, no need for a couple of tanks!' and we all burst out laughing.

The first platoon of our company, which consisted of sixty men, me included, had been ordered to set up camp at a small castle that was surrounded by vineyards. The area was called Ladutsch – or at least that's how we pronounced the name of the place. It's a small village embedded in a hilly countryside with grapevines growing up the mountain slopes and is some thirty kilometres away from Agram, which today is Zagreb. The second platoon was ordered to march on and set up in a village a kilometre further away. As for the third platoon, I can no longer remember what happened to them.

Before giving permission to enter our quarters, Lieutenant Möller, standing erect in front of us in the quadrangle, pointed out some dark spots dotted around the white-washed exterior wall: 'Listen up, everyone!' his loud voice boomed across the courtyard. 'These are blood stains. German blood. An SS unit was housed here before we arrived. Looks like their sentries must have been sound asleep and they've paid dearly for their carelessness. The partisans, mark my words, can turn up any time, any time at all! Pay attention, keep your eyes peeled, otherwise the same fate as befell the other lot – now dead – will come to you.' With that he then turned to Lieutenant Schreiner, our platoon leader: 'Divide your squad into four rotas around the clock! I am not having another incident like this mess here happen a second time!' He had barely finished with his instructions when he turned on his heels, climbed up a small flight of steps to the entrance of the castle and disappeared from view.

'Hans,' whispered Fritz, who was standing next to me. 'Looks like we'll be living in a field marshal's hall! Can you believe it – us and half of the officers under a single roof!'

'Looks like this is how it's going to be,' I responded rather wistfully. 'I'd much prefer putting my head down on a bed of straw and as far away from these gentlemen as possible.'

Then I heard the lieutenant call me, his voice loud and commanding. 'Fackler!' 'Present!' He rapidly continued down the list. 'Ziegler!' 'Present!' Four further names were called out. 'You'll take the first four hours of guard duty. See the small pavilion over there?' he asked, his finger pointing to a wooden building at the far end of the courtyard. 'From there you'll have a clear view over a large section of the road without being seen yourselves.' Making it obvious that he meant business, he added: 'I don't need to remind you of your responsibility. Dismissed!'

With our hands clutching our carbines we walked to the wooden hut. 'Shit!' is all I could hear Fritz exclaim, leaning his gun against the wall before blithely stretching himself out on the bench inside the guard room. 'Hans,' he spoke calmly, noticing my expression of shock. 'Us two and four others? Think about it, surely that's plenty guarding. The bad guys won't be paying us a visit any time soon what with their last outing being so recent. Understood? If something seems untoward, if anybody's seen passing by . . . we'll wake each other. So, you go first, have a lie-down and in two hours I'll come and get you.' Fine by me, I thought, as the way Fritz had put it seemed to me to make sense. I nodded in agreement.

Two hours later he woke me. 'Hans' he whispered. 'The moon has disappeared completely and frankly I can't see ten metres ahead of me what with all that fog.' He sounded concerned. 'You take over the street and I'll guard the courtyard.' Then, adding with increased urgency: 'This nasty weather gives me the creeps.'

Herbert Schmelig and Karl Meissner took over from us at 2200 but first showed us to the area where they had rested. 'Straw beds,' they grumbled, pointing to two empty spaces. 'The others are still awake. Curfew wasn't called until just a few minutes ago.'

Our carbines cocked, we walked to the large door, Fritz remarking on how new these surroundings felt to him. 'Do you really think the people living around here actually feel hostile towards us?'

'Well, we'll soon find out, I guess,' was my cautious reply.

The following day only the guard detail stayed at the castle, while the rest were given all sorts of tasks by the merciless corporals: crawl over marshy ground, take full cover, scale river banks, jump ditches and other pointless-seeming exercises these men came up with at a whim. By 1300, when much to our relief we caught sight of a small truck with a kitchen trailer rolling into the yard, we even had a full uniform inspection behind us. For what purpose, no one could tell, but by the time it was our turn to get our food, we looked as if we had stepped out of a band box.

'That grub in the *Gulaschkanone*,* complained Max Grünwald, 'does nothing in the slightest to lift my filthy mood. My guess is

---

* *Gulaschkanone* = 'stew gun', the nickname of the German Army's standard mobile field kitchen equipment. This was towed around in a similar manner to an artillery piece and the chimney of the stove looked a bit like a gun when it was being moved.

that all I'll do is just piss out this thin brew! No point in pretending it's a stew.' All those of us used to being around Max and knowing him as a happy-go-lucky fellow had to laugh out loud, except for Hörmann, who decided to break up the merriment with what he said was important news. 'Tomorrow,' he announced pompously, 'we may, nay, we must start work!'

'And would you, little smart-ass, also have been informed where this work will take place, or what it consists of?' someone queried, unable to hide his disdain.

'Not precisely. But rumour has it that partisans have blown up a bridge somewhere. We're to replace it with pontoons as a first step and start rebuilding it thereafter.'

'Sure sounds like a better option than slogging away around here for no good reason' I commented, which met with general approval.

It actually took surprisingly little time for most of us to become familiar with our new surroundings, and strangely we equally swiftly made contact with the locals, building up some unusual relationships. Our occasional forays into the surrounding farms to top up our meagre meals weren't exactly approved of by our superiors but to some extent were tolerated, and we took advantage of this tacit consent by adding to our daily rations fresh milk, butter, home-baked corn bread and eggs. We cared little about the protestations of the local winegrowers who thought we would take pity on their circumstances. 'German take everything – all finish! Chicken – finish! Eggs – finish! They steal pig from stable! You having salt? We not having . . . ! Maybe I thinking of good way for you.'

In the meantime, and quite fed up with the bland food offering from the *Gulaschkanone*, with its army bread and artificial honey, I had become quite creative with my menu plans, thanks above all to a food parcel from home that included some precious salt. It worked miracles with the winemakers, where I exchanged it for chicken which 'suddenly' became available, even though just a day before Germans, according to the farmers' complaints, had stolen them out of the coops. Other comrades followed suit, embarking on their own hunts, but I myself only occasionally joined these shopping excursions, accompanied by my friends, Lance-Corporals Max

Grünwald and Fritz Bauer. We had quite a jolly time observing the farmer women who went to market wearing white kerchiefs covering their hair and balancing baskets filled with their products on their heads.

One day, Max surprised me and Fritz by asking us whether we wanted to accompany him on his next outing. 'How about you two coming along with me on Sunday, that's the day after tomorrow? I'm off to a local wedding celebration.'

With us glancing at him somewhat puzzled, he just grinned and within seconds and with his inimitable youthful laughter tried to dispel any doubts we had about whether or not such an outing was indeed a sensible idea. We also couldn't quite make out how and where this invitation had come about. 'Mates,' he chuckled, 'surely, you've noticed that I disappear at nights and go visit my girlfriend. Why, didn't you all cover up for me, so nobody would notice my absence?' We actually hadn't had a clue. He got quite in his element, told us all about his adventures and proceeded to give us the full low-down of his plan.

'In her parents' house my sweetheart and I feel safe,' he assured us. 'Then, on my way home, after about a kilometre, I go through the vineyards to avoid the road.' Obviously, he had gone undetected for several days. 'Listen up! The day after tomorrow my girlfriend's sister is getting married. I've dropped plenty of hints to them that I'd bring you guys along.'

Without giving it much further thought we agreed and wouldn't you believe it: we actually ended up spending a wet but wonderful few hours celebrating with the family of Max's girlfriend. We had, on arrival, hung our own 'soldier's brides' on the stand next to our seats and had covered them up with coats, not before carefully removing the cartridges.

A number of guests of the family had filled the hall and Max tried his best to make us feel comfortable. 'Nothing,' he commented with his usual cheerful confidence, 'will happen to us here.'

Indeed, we were feeling quite at home. Each of us had brought a packet of salt to give as a present to our hosts and we enjoyed a plentiful wedding meal which I still dream about today. Putting our feet up, none of us saw any need to be shy about downing a few bottles of wine and numerous glasses of slivovitz.

It was late, perhaps already dawn, when we returned to our barracks in full view of the guards. While reporting to the morning roll call, my head still buzzing, I felt quite convinced that it all had gone unnoticed – until, that is, Sergeant Wögler passed by me and inspected my weapon. Suddenly, I was fully awake and had come to my senses.

'Are you taking the piss!' he hollered. 'What the hell are you doing with a rifle missing its bolt?'

I didn't have to look sideways but could hear that Fritz further down the line receive the same treatment. And then towards the end of the line, we could hear him flare up to a crescendo. 'Are you fucking joking? Do you think I am blind? Sort this thing at once!'

Obviously somebody had stolen the bolts from our rifles.

We had no choice but to report to our senior sergeant in his office and own up to our escapade. He was strict, but didn't seem too fussed, simply calling for the company sergeant, Sergeant-Major Oberbuchner. 'Get me the mayor of the village! Without delay!' he barked. 'I am not interested how you do it, just do it. Everything else will follow.' Pointing, but not even looking at us, he ordered: 'As for these three idiots – they are sentenced to three days' close arrest, to start immediately.' Only then did he sternly glare at each one of us individually, and with a curt 'Dismissed' he had us believing that the case for him was closed. Then came his parting words: 'Woe unto him against whom even the most minor complaint is levied! And now: Get out!'

We clicked our heels, saluted according to the rules and left the room as fast we could.

Our confinement quarters consisted of a well-preserved but empty chicken barn located behind the manor walls and constructed out of plain, unrendered bricks and a clay floor. The square windows were tiny and couldn't be opened. In the far corner of the longish room a heap of straw was ready for us to use to make up our beds.

'Well,' commented Max, broadly grinning while taking in our new quarters, 'Looks like the three of us won't suffocate in here, though the only bit of air we'll get is through this chicken chute.' And with that he settled himself on the floor as if he were back home in his comfortable house and whipped out a pack of cards from his pocket: 'Boys, forgive me for drawing you into this mess, but how on earth could I have predicted it?'

'None of us were in a state to keep an eye on our weapons throughout the evening,' Fritz offered, trying to soothe Max, who seemed more perturbed about having dragged us – his friends – into this than about the punishment.

I too didn't want the situation to get in the way of our comradeship. 'Being put on punishment for three days is not the worst thing,' I figured. 'What's more, we all had a jolly old time yesterday and enjoyed everything on offer, so let's be done with it!'

We didn't suffer one bit during our confinement. Daily, through the chicken chute, our comrades made sure to deliver us a supply of wine to top up the water rations we were receiving. Once, while we were still relishing the first drop, our mate crouching outside updated us: 'The mayor has already been to see the senior sergeant,' he began. 'But never you worry, guys ... it was a pretty tough meeting, we hear. Apparently, he gave the poor fellow a hefty what for ... you can picture it yourself.' He then expanded on the conversation that had taken place, where, he told us, the sergeant had made it abundantly clear to the mayor that if the bolts weren't returned by the following morning, every tenth male inhabitant above the age of fourteen would be shot. And, so the sergeant apparently continued, if no men were to be found in the village, then women and girls would bite the dust. The senior sergeant's parting words to the mayor were that he'd better make sure the return wasn't delayed. With that, he threw the mayor out. 'I want the three bolts back here in the barracks at the appointed deadline, and now ... get lost!' is how, so said our reporter, he had terminated the conversation.

The three of us were left in shock, including our joker who simply looked down at the floor lost in thought. The next rounds of *Skat** were played in downcast moods; nobody really felt like it. When our

---

* A popular card game.

next food and wine supply was delivered, we were pretty surprised that a good-sized chunk of lard had been thrown in along with some fresh corn bread.

'Hans, Fritz, listen!' our messenger explained through the wall. 'We took the liberty of going to speak to your salt recipients. Your rifles are complete again. We're all quite relieved that there'll be no executions . . . Our boss is no monster; he just puts on a tough face. And now, *bon appétit!*'

Towards the evening of our third day in confinement somebody unlocked the door with a loud thud and in came our senior sergeant. Even before he crossed the threshold, we slipped the last of our wine bottles under the straw, leaped up, clicked our heels and stood to attention. 'Lance-Corporal Grünwald present,' Max slurred, 'along with two men in confinement!'

With us barely able to stand upright, the sergeant bellowed: 'But the three of you are drunk!'

'Indeed, sir, indeed sergeant!' replied Max.

The sergeant's look barely concealed his disgust. 'The three of them,' he hollered towards the duty NCO still standing outside the door, 'will remain here, confined for a further three days!'

Turning again towards us he issued what seemed a last warning. 'You will regret it if I see you again in such a state!' he said sharply and turning on his heel he left the room.

The next three days passed by in pretty much the same way as those before, perhaps with a somewhat reduced supply. Nevertheless, and though our 'cell' was under constant surveillance, our comrades always succeeded in furnishing us with a few bottles of wine and carefully disposed of the empty ones.

We had barely put our confinement days behind us when we were ordered to embark on a search mission. The only information we received was unspecific but we were given to understand that Tito, the leader of the partisans, was roaming around the forest east of Agram. We were to find and arrest him or at the very least put him out of action.

The reactions before we set out came fast and furious. 'Surely you don't believe that we'll manage to do that!' 'This bugger knows too many boltholes, too many alleyways and on top of that the locals in this area are totally devoted to him!' 'This'll be a wild goose chase.'

Of course, it turned out precisely as we had imagined it would and the three-day search action proved unsuccessful. By then, winter had turned to the spring of 1944.

It has to be said that our stay would have been a very pleasant one had we not been looked upon and treated by the locals as unwanted guests, but seeing as we were the occupying forces, there was nothing we could do about it. It did, however, mean that none of us dared go out alone into the streets, and when we did venture out openly in groups we vividly sensed the hatred towards us. Only seldom did we encounter a friendly attitude and if occasionally we did receive something like a welcome, I suspect that it was put on.

One morning the telephone connection with our second platoon located in the next village not too far away from us was cut off. Our sergeant had wanted to transmit an important message to Lieutenant Zwerger, the platoon commander, but what with the unstable political atmosphere he ended up sending off not only one messenger to make personal contact, but five men in one go.

'That should suffice, I should think?' is what he apparently said to the senior sergeant before he dismissed the group, sending them on their way. They never returned. That's how far the situation had deteriorated, and nobody could feel safe any more.

One day in April 1944, I forget the exact date, we were ordered to load all our equipment onto trucks which sat waiting for us in Ladutsch and in return we were handed brand-new bicycles which we then rode in the direction of Hungary. Not a single tear was shed when we departed – by us or the inhabitants. All we Landsers wanted was to feel useful in this war, and we believed that now our moment had finally arrived. The plan to occupy and secure Hungary before the Russians had a go at it would be our chance at long last to play our part; that's at least what we were hoping for.

CHAPTER 3

Invasion of Hungary

Shortly before arriving at the Hungarian border we were ordered to hand in our bicycles and enter Hungary by truck, following behind three tanks. Apparently, we pioneers were to remove any obstacles and repair any bridges which might have been blown up or, as the case might be, needed to be erected for a proper invasion. The supply truck carrying all our equipment was behind us, but not a single shot was fired while we were en route.

Wherever we made a stop, the Hungarians greeted us warmly; children and young women would hand us bunches of flowers or welcome us with cakes and other delicacies.

'Of course, they'd do that,' observed Sepp who usually kept himself to himself. 'Compared with the Russians we must seem to them the lesser of two evils. They're about as friendly to us as folks back home are to hunters,' he added cynically. We laughed at this comparison, as we knew that Sepp lived with his parents on a small farm in Jachenau where they were employed to look after the national park and, while he didn't hold a hunting certificate, he certainly owned a gun.

It took us three days to traverse the whole of Hungary, having to spend the first night on straw beds in a gym hall somewhere in Buda. The next morning I looked on as three comrades stood outside while ferociously hurling their underwear around. Still sleepy I asked them why they seemed so agitated.

'Are you kidding! Care to take a look at your briefs and tunic? Are you perhaps the only one without lice?'

Of course, I was infested with them as well. No matter how hard we scrubbed ourselves, we just couldn't seem to free ourselves of those tiny pests – they would reappear the next day, and so went on blighting our lives. Their favourite spot seemed to be our armpits and while this was unpleasant it was, in comparison to other body parts, tolerable. Would we ever get rid of them, I asked myself?

While Hungary seemed to have been brought firmly under German control, little actually seemed to be holding us there. Once again we went through the tedious exercise of unloading our cargo only then to be quickly ordered to load it up again. Dutifully, we Landsers did as ordered. This time our journey on the freight train lasted fourteen days taking us first through Poland and then the Ukraine with frequent interruptions and long delays at random hamlets. Word of mouth had it that our destination was Kiev. At times, we were ordered to get off at some village with a small station, assemble at the local pump wells and draw water to wash ourselves, but, unfortunately as it turned out, we also used them for drinking. Some sixty men including me and eleven others from our company contracted dysentery.

Immediately on being diagnosed, we were segregated and transported to the army hospital in Lemberg* where we would spend some four weeks. I remember vividly the time when the army doctor checked me out while mumbling under his breath: 'Goodness, these are the knees of a mere boy.'

While on first impression the man seemed to be a strict sort of fellow, aloof and cold, he was no bully; on the contrary, he actually turned out to be a decent guy who made sure to keep each one of us in hospital and under his care as long as he possibly could, before he had no other option than to declare us fit for service. Once the order was issued, our return to the front would be delayed no further.

One day prior to our release from hospital, a sergeant passed my bed while blowing his nose. He apparently suffered from something called *wolinisches Fieber*.† This term meant nothing to me at the time, but by the next evening I was suffering from febrile convulsions. An older Red Cross nurse registered a fever of 41 °C, prompting her to call a doctor to my bedside. 'Another case of that *wolinisches*

---

* Now Lviv, Ukraine.
† 'Volhynia fever' was likely a form of typhus, transmitted by body lice.

Fieber,' he stated curtly and then berated the nurse. 'Why haven't you already transferred that other young man away from here . . . ? Leaving him lying here next to this emaciated beanpole', he seethed, while pointing at me, 'can't help matters.'

'Where should I have put him, for heaven's sake? We're overcrowded as it is.'

'No matter, I'll report this immediately to the chief medical officer.'

By the third day my fever had gone completely, as if it had disappeared into thin air, and I was feeling completely restored.

'Don't get too excited!' the chief medical officer warned me. 'The type of fever common round here is a treacherous one. Mark my words, it will return in full blast in another five or six days. The only remedy against it,' he explained, 'is a change of air. Then you'll get rid of it for good. Yes, come to think of it, that's exactly what I'll prescribe . . .' he said, busying himself with his notebook. 'I'll have you transferred to an army hospital in the Carpathian Mountains.' His tone was still concerned, but there was some good news – he told me that it might take a while yet for me to recover fully and once again become fit for service but that my chances of getting back on my feet were good.

After spending ten very restful days in the army hospital in the Carpathian Mountains I was given the order to report to the frontline control centre for supplies and personnel, which was located in Brünn.* As soon as I arrived and much to my surprise, rather than being sent straight on to the front, I was given sick leave and, as if this news by itself wasn't thrilling enough, my joy knew no bounds when on top of it all I was presented with a *Führerpaket*.† It contained a hard sausage, tinned meat and fish, biscuits and other food items, which all meant that I wouldn't have to arrive home to see my mum empty-handed. On my way to her I still could hear the

---

*   Now Brno, Czech Republic.
†   The *Führerpaket* was an assortment of basic foods given to soldiers going on leave to supplement their families' ration supplies. The rations would be labelled with a message such as '*Ein Kleiner Dank des Führers an seine Soldaten*' ('A little thank-you from the *Führer* to his soldiers').

words of the staff medical officer in my ears who must have taken pity on my youth: 'Get well soon!' he smiled and actually winked.

We were approaching the end of July; it was summertime and I was determined to enjoy every single minute of my furlough.

CHAPTER 4

Baptism of Fire

The days of my leave flew by as if in a dream, but then, on 12 August, came the rude awakening: I was called up to report in a hall of the Hertie department store which by that time the Wehrmacht had taken over and converted into a recruitment centre.* On inspecting my papers, a grey-haired major informed me that my unit was now positioned in the middle section of the Eastern Front and that I had better make tracks as it would take me a while to catch up with them. I was somewhat irritated at this man's pomposity, as of course I wouldn't have thought that my comrades would have moved to a place like Ingolstadt. But before I could even make a comment the man barked at me to get a move on. 'You're to depart without delay. Here are your marching papers, and now off with you!'

At that time, I didn't have the faintest idea of what it was like at the front. For that reason and actually much to my own surprise, I was filled with excited anticipation and very much looked forward to meeting up with my comrades soon. Perhaps it is hard to understand, but the warm bonds of friendship I had formed, the closeness that had developed among us and the sense of camaraderie, of belonging and of sticking together, were so strong that they didn't allow for any doubts or negative feelings.

Over the next five days I was shoved around and pushed from one distribution centre to another; nobody seemed to know the exact destination I was meant to travel to. At the train station of a small town whose name I no longer recall, a captain of the military police – we called them 'chained dogs'† because of the steel gorgets hanging

---

* The store had originally been Jewish-owned but was confiscated by the Nazis.
† *Kettenhunde* in German.

around their necks – took me on and, unusually, was helpful rather than making me more anxious as was their wont. 'There's a train for the front every twelve hours. You need to get the one at 0300 tonight,' he said and waved me away.

'Yes, captain!'

Glancing at the clock in the waiting room, I realised that I had another nine hours at my disposal and, seeing as I was dead tired, I thought I would find myself a spot where I could lie down and catch a nap until the early hours of the morning when it would be time for me to depart.

No sooner had I made my plan, than I strolled down the road leading into town where I stopped in front of a bakery from which I caught the scent of freshly baked bread. Stepping inside, I peered down at the loaves and rolls neatly arranged on the racks to my right. 'Are you looking for something specific?' asked a young and pretty sales girl standing behind the counter. 'Indeed, I would really love to have two of those crispy rolls,' I responded 'but,' I added sheepishly, 'sadly, I don't have any bread coupons.' Bread, like so many other food items, had been rationed, meaning that whenever a purchase was made the buyer had to hand over the appropriate stamps which the shop assistant would dutifully collect and hand in to the authorities. Control was of the highest priority.

'Oh well,' she said with a bemused smile, 'I'll have to do without collecting those on this special occasion ... three pieces will not raise any suspicions and it's for our soldiers. And might you want anything else?'

Emboldened by such a kind reception, I responded that in actual fact I was looking for a place to sleep. Slightly blushing, the woman told me that it so happened that the bed of their apprentice was not occupied. 'He's at the Western Front, you see, and we still haven't replaced him. You're welcome to sleep in his room provided our good master doesn't object.'

And because it turned out that the good master didn't mind at all, I had a wonderfully restful sleep and, of course, missed the specified 0300. With no other option, I found myself sat in the station's waiting room just before 1500 when I spotted the captain from the previous day, accompanied by two of his 'chained dogs', I tried hiding behind the large back of the person sitting next to me, but no sooner had I moved, than the chained dog's piercing eyes spotted me. He marched straight up to me, fuming. 'Have you gone mad,' he barked, 'you were supposed to have cleared out of here this morning! There will be consequences!' Gone was his previous good will.

Standing erect in front of the incensed man, I could still see from the corner of my eye the captain jotting something down in his note book. While I wondered to myself what he could possibly be writing, he ripped out the page and handed it to me, his face flushed with anger. 'You're to give this note to the captain of your company. The train is pulling in right now. Get yourself on it. You can count yourself lucky that you've got off so lightly. Beat it!'

It was only once I had settled down in the train that I could make myself read the note: 'I hereby punish you with three days of harsh arrest because you did not use the prescribed train at 0300 and have remained here an additional twelve hours. Signed: Captain Krüger.' It goes without saying that this note never reached its intended addressee.

After six days of travel the train came to a halt in the middle of a field, right next to a wooden shed. 'All men off the train! Final stop!' I heard someone shout. I certainly felt the worse for wear.

I was allowed to continue my journey atop a truck which took me some twenty kilometres further east only then, for the last bit of the trip, to be put on a small horse-drawn cart where I shared the narrow bench with the driver. That small horse, obviously not one of our German breeds, briskly trotted along with his thick mane shaking in the wind and me shaking with every metre we put behind us as the roads were badly paved and the cart wheels worn out. The coachman was a Hiwi.*

When we stopped alongside a narrow path that led into a small forest the driver motioned me to get off. Jumping to the ground, my

---

* Hiwi was an abbreviation for *Hilfswilliger* meaning 'voluntary assistant'. These were Soviet citizens, usually former prisoners of war, who had enlisted in the German forces and performed both non-combatant and combatant tasks.

legs stiff from the cold, I felt quite lost. The driver, a stick-thin man of around thirty who only spoke a broken German, motioned me to continue my journey on foot.

'You . . . up to top. Always attention: good cover. Russians shooting very good . . . Very far. Your company after this small forest, in trench. Later, in night, I bringing food.'

He had already pulled the reins for his cart to turn nearly full circle and he was gone.

Some fifteen minutes later I reached the front line having made my way through a well-camouflaged communications trench. Picking my way through the men, I couldn't spot a single recognisable face. A light fog hovered over the countryside, somewhat obscuring my view when I tried peering over the edge of the ditch so I struggled to make out the Russians who were encamped some 500 metres away from us. A Landser whom I didn't know at the time quickly pulled me back. 'So young,' he said with reproach in his voice, 'and already tired of life? Why, comrade, don't you know that those Ivans over there will just zap you within seconds?' Realising he had shocked me, he softened his tone. 'They're excellent marksmen,' he added, 'so just do yourself a favour and keep your head down. Your helmet isn't bullet-proof.' Slightly bent over and shaking his head, he stomped on through the trench.

At long last I stumbled on some comrades I knew from before and who recognised my voice. Crawling out from under bushes and from holes covered by branches and leaves they encircled me, warmly shook my hand and thumped my back. Looking at their bearded and drawn faces I became conscious of what my friends must have gone through while I had been on furlough. 'Well, look at our adventurer!' exclaimed our usually taciturn sniper from Jachenau who was the first to find his voice. 'Here he is then, a true expert survivor . . . seems to have found us at long last after his little rest at the army hospital.'

But my delight at being once more reunited fast disappeared when I was informed that Josef Sillinger from Augsburg, 'king' of Pfaffenhausen near Ilm, had been killed and, sadder still, that I had lost both my 'cell mates' from Croatia, Fritz and Max.

'Hans,' added one comrade in a hushed tone, 'Can you believe it, our old captain also got caught out, it must have been a fortnight ago . . . The leader of what remains of our troupe is Lieutenant Hartmann. He's okay. You may remember him from back in Croatia.' I couldn't quite take it all in and must have looked stunned. 'Why don't you report to him and he'll probably allocate you to the section in charge of laying mines . . .' My comrade urged me out of my momentary stupor – 'that's where us lot work. Seems to be the only way to keep the Russians from chasing us away from here.'

And indeed, it turned out just as he had predicted. That was the section I was deployed to. That night, in the pitch dark, five other men and me clambered out of our shelters, making quite sure to leave our paybooks stored in our company command post which would, should it come to pass that we were taken prisoner, dead or alive, make it impossible for the enemy to identify us or our past record.

Some fifty metres away from the German trenches, in so-called no-man's-land, the mines, meant for our own protection, were to be buried beneath the surface. As quietly as possible, using only our short shovels, we dug round holes and small pits, adjusting our technique to what type of mine we had been supplied with. 'Above all, don't make a noise!' whispered my comrade from Jachenau into my ear not before mumbling into his jacket but clear enough for me to hear: 'I wish I was back in my own hole already, under my blanket.'

'Don't pay too much attention to him,' countered Hans Obermaier. 'He's scared that at the faintest sound the Russians will set off one of their magical fireworks displays.'

'Ha! Surely he must know that our men won't do anything provocative around here what with us laying out this carpet of ours,' yet another one of our guys interjected.

'Stop it right now! Not a single word from any of you. The Russians could be closer than we think.' Corporal Huber was annoyed.

Each one of us then kneeled or crouched over his device busily doing his job, planting a piece of land with mines rather than seeds and leading to destruction rather than growth. At times we would also connect two explosives with a trip wire to cause greater harm.

We were acutely aware that one single incorrect move could mean instant death and worked silently.

My heart was in my mouth but I controlled my nerves while we cautiously inched forward. Working from the far left of the field then across to the other side, we were completely absorbed in our task, planting mine after mine, when suddenly the crack of a Russian machine gun breaking through the still and foggy night tore us out of our routine. Immediately my comrades lay close to the ground, with me the last one to take full cover as I had hesitated for just a few moments. Why make such a fuss in the face of just a bit of shooting I thought to myself, when promptly a bullet whooshed past above my head just barely missing me.

We kept low for a bit longer and, though our insides were shaking, we were careful not to make a move and only when calm seemed to settle once more did we continue with our painstaking work. After two interminable hours labouring away in our deadly assembly line – two comrades supplied the new mines which we would then skilfully conceal – we descended back into our shelters. When I was about to step down, Corporal Huber, grabbing my arm, held me back and took me to our MG position only a few metres away.

A sniper kneeling behind the heavy MG, which was clamped onto a fixed mount, fired off an entire cartridge belt's worth of ammunition, seemingly unperturbed by us joining him.

'This good chap,' Corporal Huber remarked, pointing to the kneeling soldier, 'was waiting for us.' 'At last light', he continued, 'he made quite sure that it was pointing in the right direction and then properly clamped it all down – so no need for him to get all fussed now about whether or not he's hitting the target . . . he knows he will.' The corporal seemed quite nonchalant. 'Yup, he's fully on the ready to carpet the entire area over there with his blessings. And believe you me, those guys on the other side don't do it any differently. But one more point,' his tone now more concerned, 'you must make sure to take cover as swiftly as you've just seen us do – as you'll remember from our training.'

He threw something approximating a smile at me and finished his personal induction by wishing me a good night's rest. 'Make sure to wrap up warmly and sleep as long as they'll allow us. Why don't you lie yourself down next to Jürgen over there. Look, he's already waving for you to join him.'

There we were, encamped for some fourteen days, close to a small forest on the outskirts of Kiev. Though the Russians made several attempts to penetrate our line they invariably failed at each attack and while all we had directly at our disposal in terms of weapons were mortars and small arms, our artillery was precise and more often than not the Russians were getting their heads blown off.

We were not spared either. I saw comrades in the unit right next to us crumpling into a heap on the ground, hit by 'friendly' shellfire; tanks went up in flames and I witnessed silhouettes in uniforms of an earthy brown colour on the other side being shredded apart or mutilated in front of my eyes. I can still recall how their shouts of *'Urrah!'* gradually faded until they fell silent. I felt compassion for these fellows who weren't any older than us lads.

By the time when it came to the second or third attack, I felt increasingly numb. The fierce shelling from all directions, ricochets whirling in the air – the cacophony of noise left me with a feeling of shock. Had I, I asked myself, perhaps inevitably grown accustomed to the carnage? Had I become immune? Death was commonplace and it no longer mattered whether it was them or us. It was only when I had a quiet moment to myself that I had the time or the energy to reflect and to question the meaning of it all. Finding no answer, I resigned myself to focusing on and being mindful of not coming to harm. It was madness. The feelings of excitement I fully enjoyed while in the training camp had made way for something hard to describe; perhaps it was something akin to sobering dis-illusionment.

To protect our positions, we were instructed night after night to climb out of our trenches and plant ever more mines in no-man's-land and this too became routine. But one morning we had a rude awakening, though few of us ever actually slept well. The Red Army had encircled the area our units were encamped in and, as they fired one rocket volley after another at us, we barely managed to dash for cover into our bolt holes. Ducking in our trenches for what seemed an age we expected further attacks, but while nothing happened, the rumour that Ivan had penetrated our defence line on both the right and left-hand side circulated rapidly.

We were ordered to withdraw. Bursting with admiration for our leader, Lieutenant Hartmann, who had a remarkable way of issuing commands with exceptional composure, we withdrew in a calm, orderly fashion, avoiding the awful predicament of having to leave behind precious equipment or weapons. By dawn our positions were deserted: we had abandoned them quietly but swiftly, making sure not to alert the enemy to our intentions. Much to our surprise, however, it didn't seem as if the enemy was in any rush to chase us. This disconcerted us somewhat. But our superiors maintained we had nothing to fear. At one point during our withdrawal, I heard the lieutenant call across to Corporal Huber that Ivan had bet on the wrong horse. 'We're no easy prey, us lot!' he remarked with pride in his voice.

I couldn't quite catch what Huber responded but after being ordered to get a move on, I thought it best to obey him without commenting.

We then moved back from the front line, occupying a reception camp, temporary and woefully ill-equipped but where we were able to remain undetected for long enough to catch our breath, without running the risk of being surrounded by the enemy. This is how it continued day after day, dodging Ivan, marching for hours with hardly any rest, and when granted a short one we were so exhausted that we could barely stay upright. Simply collapsing onto the floor, some fell asleep instantly, others preferred to sit and talk a while.

During one such rest period our sniper from Jachenau who was lying next to me felt like chatting, probably hoping for my reassurance. 'Hans, what does this bode for us? Are we about to become prisoners of war? Mark my words, if it actually comes to that, I'd rather put a bullet through my head beforehand. That will be a quicker death than pegging out in a POW camp.'

'Oh man,' I tried to calm him down. 'Why paint it all so bleak? All we have to do is run faster until such time as we've straightened out this blasted front line.'

I am not sure whether it was on the third or fourth day of our withdrawal that I suddenly became aware of a sergeant-major whom I had never seen before standing next to Lieutenant Hartmann. They seemed to be talking as if old friends. Leaning with his back relaxing against the sidecar of his DKW the sergeant rested his helmet with the motorbike glasses strapped around it on the driver's saddle. Studying his face with its sharp features and his erect stature, I estimated him to be only some thirty years old, yet judging from the various medals sewn onto his army jacket I gathered that this was a seasoned fighter.

Suddenly I saw Lieutenant Hartmann waving me to approach. Obviously referring to the newly arrived visitor, Hartmann informed me that the sergeant had asked him to select a strong and fearless soldier who would assist him on his special mission. 'You're the man I am putting forward,' he said which I took for what he obviously meant as a compliment. 'We're breaking camp and the company is heading out straight away to our next position. Meanwhile, you'll be staying put alongside this good officer and forming the rearguard to protect us. Good luck, Fackler – both to you and to us all.'

My company did indeed march off, but marching is not the correct term if I'll be honest as the column I saw disappearing into the distance bore little resemblance to what I knew to be a German unit. Looking at the line of grey men filing past, it brought to mind a worm of weary and exhausted bodies stumbling along mindlessly. And yet, I felt utterly devastated when I gradually lost sight of them.

Eyeing me curiously the sergeant studied my reactions. 'I'm Hannes,' he finally introduced himself, asking me for my name.

'Hans.'

'Good. Let's agree on this one straight off the bat: no way we'll allow the Russians to come past us.'

He was obviously much amused by the puzzled look I must have thrown in his direction as he burst out laughing before explaining himself. 'Just thank your lucky stars that you no longer have to be doing this on foot, Hans. My plan is for you to hop onto my bike and we'll follow the others slowly, careful to keep our distance, so that the Russians will catch a glimpse of us only from behind and only now and then. I've got plenty of fuel and I'll keep you abreast of everything, never you worry.' He seemed confident of his strategy. 'Look at it from the bright side, young lad, it's something a bit different for the likes of you.'

I hadn't had a cigarette for two whole days. My new comrade, and I never doubted that this is what I could indeed consider him to be, noticed the longing look in my eyes as I stood watching him as he turned the Eckstein packet on its head and knocked out a cigarette for himself. He then offered one to me. The prestigious brand said it all. He was a real officer, and a generous one at that. 'I've plenty more where that came from,' he grinned. Eagerly I took some deep puffs, exhaling with relish, and my eyes closed but I then became quite dizzy. 'Take it easy, young man. You're not supposed to devour it – just slow down, enjoy it. You'll see the difference – you'll feel relaxed in no time.'

I sure needed something to calm my nerves as truth be told I felt totally lost being stranded there alone with Hannes, nobody around us and in the middle of the plain. But, keen not to give myself away, I did all I could to appear as nonchalant as my new companion.

Without being prompted he began to speak about himself. He had been a groom in a stables before the war had broken out and, as it turned out, not just anywhere or for just anybody. His employer was General von Bonstein whose vast estate lay near Königsberg. 'What I had dreamed about,' he went on wistfully, 'was to become the estate steward.' But things would turn out differently, he mumbled more to himself than for my benefit. 'They called me up and I joined "Prussia's Glory".'* With his shoulders now slightly bent, he looked down and his thoughts abruptly returned to the present. 'If the Russians advance as far as that, woe betide our wives and children!'

Quickly shaking off his momentary feeling of depression he straightened up and, fortunately for me, returned to his old self. I felt it only polite to let him know a bit about myself and so chatted about my days at the RAD, about the air attacks on my home town, and

---

* '*Preußens Gloria*' was a military march tune, and by extension a slang term for the German Army.

before we knew it some four or five hours had gone by. Suddenly my comrade's face tensed up and I immediately stopped blabbing away. Engine noise was steadily coming closer. Could it be that the Russian tanks had caught up with us? Without either one of us uttering a word I just followed Hannes' finger pointing to the sidecar and squeezed myself in as best I could while he was already on his seat pushing down on the pedals and revving up the engine. He seemed to know precisely the route we needed to take; while we had been jabbering about this and that, it hadn't escaped me that he had pulled out a folded map from his leather briefcase which he had then studied, all the while continuing the conversation. Shouting through the air and above the noise of the engine he yelled that it was only 15 kilometres to the Dniestr. 'Mark my words, our Lieutenant Hartmann and friends are busy getting the bridge over the river ready just in time to welcome Ivan.'

When I threw him a questioning look, he just grinned sideways down at me and chuckled: 'Hans, listen to me, one thing these iron clods of Stalin's haven't learned is how to swim. The bridge will be blown up and guess who'll be doing that?' Without expecting an answer, he explained: 'The two of us, of course.'

And it so it came to pass that this former groom whom I had met only a few hours earlier sped along the dead-straight path with me beside him heading westward and determined to meet the enemy advance head-on. It took us the predicted quarter of an hour until we hit the bridge. While we thundered across it I was just able to catch a glimpse of the still water underneath. Once we had reached the shore on the other side, Hannes came to an abrupt stop. 'Just stay put for a few moments!' he ordered, dismounted from his bike and ran up the embankment towards some shrubbery fifty metres further up the street. Returning straight away, he assured me that all was fine. 'Your comrades have done all the prep work. Excellent. We have a perfect view, yet cannot be seen and luckily, it looks like we've been granted a clear escape route,' he assured me, turning his head up to the bushes. 'Under the bridge we'll find some stuff to detonate,' he explained, 'cute little explosives and, wham, we're going to give the Russians a firework display which sure won't be what they fancy.'

All I could do was nod vigorously and marvel at how the cockiness of my new acquaintance felt so contagious. Without losing another moment, sarge swung himself back onto his bike, slowly rode along the shrubbery he had identified before and continued on the road until it reached a forest. Steadying himself on the footrests, he lifted his lanky body and turned around. 'Hans,' he exclaimed, obvious satisfaction swinging in his voice, 'this here seems made to measure for us. After all is done and dusted, we can dash off and drive right up to here without brother Ivan ever catching sight of us from the other side of the river.'

While I scrambled out of the passenger sidecar, he nodded towards my rifle. 'May as well leave it behind, it'll just get in your way. But give me a hand, will you, we need to dress up our vehicle here, so that the Russians cannot spot it from above either, in case they're sending a reconnaissance aircraft our way ... Let's get some branches and greenery.' Then we dug out a hole and waited. 'They won't turn up in a hurry,' the sergeant said with utmost certainty, and encouraged me to remain patient and trusting. 'Hartmann has planted loads of tank mines in two particular areas along the road – I know that as a fact – that'll keep them busy for a while. I can tell you one thing: you sure lucked out with your lieutenant.' Yes, he was most definitely spot on with his judgement, I thought.

To my mind, time crawled by literally at a snail's pace. Meanwhile I had the sarge crouching beside me with a square-shaped tin box in front of him, covered in a net-like metal fabric from which protruded a round metal rod with a T-shaped tip. The moment sarge moved that pin while pressing it down, a current would flow from a battery through the wire, trigger the igniters and set off the explosion. But would all this work out, I wondered? That worry kept playing on my mind, over and over again, while both of us were closely observing the road on the other side of the river.

Some six tense hours went by and it was afternoon. I was just about to light myself a cigarette when I felt the officer's hand on my arm. Jerking his chin up and ahead, he didn't utter a word. That's when I, too, narrowing my eyes, gazed ahead and spotted the first tank with others following, one rolling after the other across the terrain.

Seconds later and I could clearly make out Russian infantry winding in and out among those monstrosities. I suddenly felt queasy. Never before had I actually come face to face with the enemy, and they were all armed to the teeth. Naked fear must have stared out of my eyes.

'Keep still, my boy. I am right beside you, Hans. None of them knows how to swim.' Sarge's voice was as calm as if he'd just exchanged some pleasantries at a social gathering while sitting comfortably in the armchair of a living room.

Once the first T-34 had reached the ramp leading up to the bridge we could make out the distinct crunching and clanging noises of the tank tracks mixed with the roar of the engines. But what was that? As if given orders by a ghost, the entire column came to an abrupt halt. Further down the line, I could see Russian infantrymen slipping away to the sides and taking cover right and left of the street. Then, I noticed the tank hatch being opened and out peeked the head of the commander with his cap on. Plain for me to see, he was holding a pair of binoculars to his eyes and I instinctively ducked further down into my hole.

'Nothing to fear,' Hannes assured me. 'We're well camouflaged – the bozo can't see anyone, let alone hear anything.'

Convinced that the sound of my pounding heart could be heard far and wide I could barely remain focused. 'Hans, just watch, it'll all happen in seconds. The first one is rolling. Oh . . . but the others don't seem to be following him!' Sarge sounded disappointed. But he kept his steel-blue eyes on the gigantic iron beast about to cross. When the first Russian tank had just about reached the middle of the bridge, I could feel a jolt going through Hannes's body and, stunned, watched how he calmly turned the handle while pressing it down. 'Many happy returns!' he shouted.

Fixated on what would happen next, I more or less instantly heard the deafening sound of the explosion ripping through the air, followed by bridge parts being flung far in every direction as if a huge fountain had been turned on spraying brown water shoots. I could hardly believe my eyes when, from the force of the detonation, the gigantic tank was lifted into the air about one metre high and then plunged into the waters, main gun first.

'Away!' barked the sergeant and I sure didn't need to hear that twice. We sprinted off and before we even reached our bike, shells hit the very spot we had just vacated. Chattering bursts of fire followed, dangerously missing us by just a few inches. We quickly tore away the branches covering our vehicle and sped off.

Some 100 metres behind us shells continued blasting into the ground but Hannes and I had succeeded in our mission. 'Good man, we made it!' he exclaimed triumphantly.

After a few kilometres we reached the far end of the forest and, continuing across fields, we finally entered a small hamlet which sarge initially intended to go straight through. There was not a soul nor sausage to be seen. Well, to be precise, we did see a few pigs cross the road right in front of us. 'Fancy catching one for the slaughter?' I shouted up to Hannes.

'No way, it'll only be the rats who'll enjoy it, this stuff is riddled with worms. Let's get a move on!'

Suddenly I felt a jolt – Hannes had pushed hard on the brakes. We pulled up at the front of a German warehouse – it was clearly signposted – with its portals wide open and seemingly inviting us to have a good look inside.

'Goodness me, and who do we have here?' Sarge had noticed the quartermaster sitting at his table at the very end of the long corridor. 'Bit of a surprise, that, seeing as these yokels are usually known to set fire to their place and then be the first to scram. Well, what of it? We sure must make good use of our time. Come with me!' he gestured for me to follow him. 'Let's have a look-see for what we can put our hands on.'

On entering what was quite a low building, we could see on the right-hand side shelves reaching up to the corrugated metal roof filled with neatly piled-up uniforms, underwear and armaments. But the other side was of greater interest to us. Tons of the Wehrmacht's solid staples were staring straight at us, there for the taking. Tinned meat and fish jars, bags of sugar and salt and lots more. Just as I was busily filling my empty gasmask box with several round canisters of so-called aviator chocolate and then stuffing in for good measure a few packs of cigarettes, the burly quartermaster finally rose from his seat and shuffled towards us in a leisurely way. 'There'll be no pilfering on my watch,' he growled.

'Keep your trap shut!' was Hannes's response. 'What's wrong with you? D'you intend to leave it all to the Russians? Go to it, set it all on fire – now! We're the last Germans you'll get to see here. Behind us,' he waved his arm over his shoulder, 'the enemy is en route! It'll take them no time to build a temporary bridge!' he shouted as the guy was still not budging and didn't seem to believe a word Hannes was saying to him. 'To the right and left of us the Russians have already pushed through! Now, buddy. I'm not planning to discuss this with you for one more minute and I'll be taking whatever I can put to good use!' I really thought that Hannes had made himself quite clear and that we were done.

'No,' said the quartermaster obstinately, 'there is no plundering on my turf, and if there is, it'll be over my dead body.'

'Then so be it!'

Hannes pulled his Luger pistol from its holster and shot. The quartermaster, not a young man judging by his already greying hair, was lying on the floor before I could blink. His hand was on his Walther pistol but there was a circular hole in the middle of his forehead – there he was sprawled out three or four metres away from us, his cap next to him. I was deeply shaken and actually upset.

'Oh, man, come to, will you,' Hannes somewhat brusquely tried to placate me. 'All I actually did was take this poor sod out of certain misery. The Russians would have tortured him to death, slowly and painfully. And now,' he spoke sternly, 'come along. We must catch up with your lot as quickly as we can.'

I never found out what my East Prussian comrade had helped himself to and frankly, I didn't actually care.

All I saw was that after I plucked some hand grenades out of the storage, he also grabbed a few, bunched them together in his fist and hurled it as a single concentrated charge into the farthest part of the hall. Within seconds a fire had broken out followed by a deafening explosion.

While I was shaken by the brutal death of the quartermaster, my comrade didn't seem to be troubled one bit. We drove off, each one keeping his thoughts to himself. Only once did he stop to study the map.

The sun had just about disappeared behind the western horizon when I reported back to Lieutenant Hartmann. Hannes, meanwhile, departed, travelling to an unknown destination. As for me, I felt that I had arrived back 'home', my comrades thumping me on my back with undisguised appreciation for what we had achieved.

CHAPTER 5

Retreats and Wounds on the Eastern Front

Three or four days later found us setting up camp just between two hills, in a hollow. Rumour had it that the front line had been straightened out, but then again, who knew what was really going on, as we Landsers wouldn't have been privy to any precise information in any event. I couldn't quite tell whether Lieutenant Hartmann himself didn't have any details to share with us or whether he was just keeping them close to his chest. Perhaps, he too was being kept in the dark like the rest of us? What happened next, though, was nothing short of a miracle.

After being allowed to take a brief rest we were joined by a bunch of some fifteen replacements– all young and fresh-cheeked lads who had recently been dispatched from the barracks in Germany. There were also about three regular guys among them who had just been released from field hospitals. Given the order to dig out some defence positions on the hill to the east of us and get the sap going, we were just about to start climbing up when a Kübelwagen rolled across the field heading in our direction.

Without even alighting from his vehicle, a Luftwaffe colonel beckoned Lieutenant Hartmann to approach and handed him some papers. Only then did he jump to the ground to address the rest of us. 'As of now I am your company commander.' His statement boded ill. 'And goodness gracious! Look at the sight of you slovenly bunch! No one has shaved!' More was to come. 'We're not a band of hooligans!' he hollered. 'This pig sty needs to be cleaned up instantly and, read my lips, I'll make this happen!' Launching straight from berating us about our looks – I mean where the hell were we supposed to have cleaned up – he set about reconfiguring the structure that Hartmann had put in place. 'Listen up: not a single one of us is to be seen up there on the hill. We will be building our rear positions right here. There is a reason for that! Dismissed!'

Though we were seasoned soldiers and accustomed to obeying orders without questioning them, we sensed that there was something wrong with this man and we just looked at each other perplexed. Why would anyone appear from nowhere and just bully us around? Forming small clusters while walking away, we tried to figure out what this was all about.

'The man's out of his mind!'

'Where did he get off?'

'All we needed was a twit like him!'

'With the Russians firing from the top, we'll be cannon fodder. Haven't we suffered sufficient losses?'

While moaning and groaning, we heard several shots fired behind us. A few metres away from us lay the dead colonel. We sure weren't the only ones gobsmacked. Standing right next to the dead body was a stunned Lieutenant Hartmann staring down at the red bloodstains which slowly seeped through the colonel's jacket. Much to our surprise, the lieutenant didn't ask a single question as to what might have happened. 'Listen up! As of right now you're back under my orders!' is all he shouted. 'Everything back to how it was before and how it was discussed. We're digging ourselves in up there.'

'Absolutely, all that would happen to us down here is total extermination!' somebody commented from the back.

'Shut your trap! That's enough.'

From the top of the hill we could survey the area far across towards the east with our view only slightly hampered by a few houses situated some 600 metres away from what would be our shelter. Somewhere over there, we figured, the Russians were lying in wait, though much as we craned our necks, we couldn't see a single human being. Or perhaps they hadn't come that far yet? No harm in hoping, we told ourselves.

I had been assigned a few metres to dig out and I started straight away. The intention was, of course, that we not just build any old random defence but that, importantly, we ensure that MG nests be strategically concealed in pits. Corporal Huber joined in while supervising and encouraging us on. 'Well done, looking good and solid. Looks like we'll be spending some considerable time up here.' He obviously enjoyed having us under his command once again and the incident was forgotten.

Several men digging near us had located some heavy beams and after dragging them to site let them drop to the ground with a thud. 'Gosh, where did these come from?' we asked with obvious envy, briefly pausing to catch our breath.

'Found them down there below, where we discovered a smashed-up farmhouse. Methinks we'll pay it another visit and be back in a moment.'

By lunch time I had excavated quite a bit of my dugout and what with my back hurting and having lost interest in this task of ours, I decided to call it a day. 'Hey Richard, listen!' I called out to my comrade working next to me pointing to the houses mentioned before. 'Surely nobody'll mind if we take a closer look at our surroundings.'

'And right you are,' was his jovial response and on he went chewing on his pipe that for a long time hadn't seen any tobacco. Richard's home was in the Oberpfalz and I'll always treasure the memory of him as a solidly decent fellow. He always wanted to do it by the book, so to speak. 'I think we'd better tell Huber,' he suggested. 'We'll simply say that we're doing some reconnaissance.'

After a few minutes we set off at a leisurely pace approaching the first house. Shortly before arriving, I realised that I had left my rifle back at the trench, right next to where I had been digging, perhaps one or two metres away from the section I had excavated. Too lazy to walk back, I just mentioned it to Richard. 'No worries,' he replied without removing the pipe from his mouth. 'I've got mine and one should be enough.'

Turning the corner to reach the front entrance, we stopped short. The dead bodies of two Landsers were lying prostrate in front of us.

'Looks like the Russians have already arrived,' mumbled Richard taking the gun from his shoulder.

'Shit,' I swore, 'I'd have expected anything but that. All looked so peaceful from up there.'

Cautiously, trying not to make a sound, we crept through the house from room to room, but didn't see any sign that somebody had actually recently been there. On we went to the next house, a sort of German depot but everything had been removed, all except for some brand new rifles to one of which I helped myself immediately, loading it with some of Richard's spare bullets. This instantly made us feel more comfortable. No longer seeing the need to investigate the place further, we slid back to the first house, climbed up to the attic and peeped through the tiny dormer window. This time round it was not for nothing. At a distance of about 200 metres, we could make out several khaki-grey coloured silhouettes moving around. There was no mistaking, we muttered to ourselves. The Russians had indeed arrived.

'They don't do things by half,' mumbled Richard under his breath. 'We call them barbarians, but you've got to give it to them . . . they've set up home there and we didn't have a clue.'

'Richard, we'll need to report this instantly.' With the words barely out of my mouth, we were flung back by the impact of a round smashing into the walls. Stumbling downstairs we could see a cloud of chalk dust coming out of a hole through which we scrambled to the outside. Running back to our unit we could hear more cracking noises of shells exploding, both of us convinced they were Russian ones.

When we told Huber, he smirked, raising his eyebrows. 'Russian artillery?' he puffed. 'Only you two nincompoops can believe such nonsense. Let me set you straight,' he continued, 'our men out there are flanking the enemy. Some idiot killed two, injured three – that's friendly fire for you. We sure could do without such nonsense!' he added, clearly annoyed – whether at us, or at us as the proverbial messengers bearing bad news, I couldn't figure out.

After a moment's consideration, however, he must have decided that he needed to relay the incident to his superior. 'Will have a word with Hartmann. Seems to me that we'd better bring the corpses back to us.'

Returning to our stretch, I was dismayed to realise that our previous dugouts had been turned into shell craters and my carbine flung to the side, smashed into smithereens. 'What did I say? Seems like our little excursion has paid off,' grinned Richard.

'Boy oh boy, we just about got away with it!'

After a short while Huber returned from his report to Hartmann. 'We're not allowed to leave our two dead Germans to the Russians. Hartmann wants to find out which unit it was that has fled. You're familiar with the area – go find them!'

About an hour later a small cart appeared seemingly out of nowhere – nobody questioned where or how the vehicle was found, but it was ours from then on and several of us set off to fetch the dead bodies. Relying on the house that offered at least some protection against any Russian guard posts, none of us felt especially concerned or even apprehensive. We sure were wrong. The enemy didn't sleep. Though we tried to remain out of sight, rifle grenades came whizzing straight by us fragmenting into a maelstrom of shards and splinters. By sheer luck we were able to bring the dead bodies back – ourselves unscathed.

Much to our amazement the sergeant was expecting us. Standing next to a freshly dug pit some hundred metres behind the trenches and ready to receive the corpses, he requested we hand him the infantrymen's paybooks and remove their boots – those weren't allowed into their grave.

'Where did you get this lovely light birchwood?' I asked Huber when he was about to place the modest cross into the earth mound.

'From the forest, dimwit!'

'All I could see there were thick tree trunks.' 'Sure,' replied Huber smugly. 'but branches grow thinner at the far end ... common knowledge.' 'Not keen on them in any event,' commented Richard morosely. Like the rest of us his mood had deteriorated to a dangerous extent owing to the grim circumstances we were facing, not helped by the ice-cold October wind whistling about our ears and bringing some early snow flurries.

'Shit. The weather has turned. That's all we need,' grumbled Huber into his beard stubble while leading the way to our trenches, which had in the meantime already been camouflaged with planks and branches.

As one supposedly familiar with the terrain, Hartmann sent me back the following morning to the first house to observe the area from its dormer window. Requesting that I take along an old chum of mine as well as one who had just recently joined, he briefed us. 'Should you notice anything untoward, anything you suspect to be a threat, you're to notify me instantly.'

'Yes, sir!'

'Off with you! And no unnecessary escapades!'

'No, sir.'

Minutes later the novice and myself stood at the dormer window, while we could hear Heinz Burger below us examining the rooms but being careful only to tread softly on the floorboards. I made quite sure to exhale the smoke of my cigarette sideways, thus not allowing it to escape through the window and give us away.

Our newcomer seemed anxious and so I did all I could think of to distract him.

'Where are you from, Horst?' I asked him.

'From Potsdam.'

'Really, and here you are, one of us, in the middle section of our mountain division! By the way, I say mountain division, but, look at us . . . our riflemen jokingly call us the flatland division.'

'I didn't volunteer for this division,' was his sour retort.

'Hardly any of us did.'

Suddenly Heinz appeared up in the attic dragging behind him an old record player. It was one of those wooden boxes with a winding key on the side with which one could crank up the inside motor allowing several records to drop down in turn onto the rotating turntable. Everything seemed to be in working order, including the taper tube with the needle and the sound box attached to it. And lo and behold, what did Heinz carry under his other arm? A carton filled with a whole bunch of records.

'Are those Russian records?'

'Nope, already looked at them,' replied Heinz, obviously pleased with his booty. 'They're Richard Tauber, *Zar und Zimmermann* and suchlike.* Someone must have just left them behind.' All we need to do is crank up the box and put the needle on the grooves of a record.

'But where did you find all this?' I asked, sensing that this might cause problems with our superiors.

'Was just lying over there,' Heinz waved his arm in no particular direction. 'Just stumbled over them when I picked up a few guns left in a corner.'

'Heinz, listen closely, think of Hartmann's warning. We can't afford any more escapades.'

'Bullshit! Why, of course we wouldn't rub his nose in it – we'll just keep it to ourselves. By the way, I've also put my name on a pair of solid felt boots. You probably didn't spot these warm "padders" the first time round. Before we return, you'd be smart to help yourself. But try them on first. Think about it – we're not getting anything put in our laps – and they're just lying around here.' He got into his element. 'What we should be doing is spreading the word. Wouldn't you think that others would also want to spruce up their uniforms? And their equipment? Believe me, once it turns cold, we'll sure be glad about our new gear.'

'Goodness, Heinz! You're dead right, I'll get myself a pair right this minute.'

'Just hold on! Let's first offer those guys there on the other side some entertainment.'

Before I could contradict or reject his idea, he intoned the song '*Es steht ein Soldat am Wolgastrand, hält Wache für sein Vaterland . . .*'† and though it was very moving, the tranquillity of the morning had been disturbed.

Something just didn't seem right to me and I couldn't help scanning the area with my eyes eventually focussing on some shrubbery about 150 metres away from the house in what was once probably a neatly maintained garden alongside the street. My hunch

---

* Richard Tauber was an acclaimed Austrian tenor. Of Jewish ancestry, he lived in Britain during the war. *Zar und Zimmermann* is an opera, music by Albert Lortzing.

† The song 'A soldier stands on the bank of the Volga' is from Franz Lehár's operetta *The Tsarevich*.

was that this is where the Russian outpost lay in waiting, hidden away within a burrow. Would they react?

'Heinz!' I could literally feel Horst's anxiety by the way he called out his name. 'If they decide to clean us out, we'd better clear out first!'

'I'm not bothered,' said Heinz nonchalantly and this seemed to have done the trick for Horst who had been gripping his gun so hard that his knuckles had turned white. He eventually loosened his hold, relaxed a bit and the three of us burst out laughing.

What then unfolded strangely reinforced our own impressions about what at that stage of the war appeared to us as its senselessness: the tragedy of lives lost, and the stereotype of the enemy we had believed in. We could see an arm appearing on the other side, the coloured uniform sleeve was clearly visible, and it was waving to us in an obviously friendly greeting. Squinting, we could even make out a fresh-faced boy wearing a Russian steel helmet.

'Bob's your uncle!' exclaimed Heinz with his winning grin. 'Problem solved!'

'But only for as long as no superior butts in and puts an end to this.'

'Ha, you're right there, but not before each one of us gets his grubby hands on a pair of felt boots.'

We spent some eight days up there in the attic feeling safe and contented – very nearly at home. And it was warm. The Russians, as far as we could tell at least, must have felt much the same. Watching them as they crept in and out of their burrows, replacing their double sentries at regular intervals based on what we had counted to be a total of ten to twelve men, they seemed unconcerned, going about their usual business and blithely obeying routine instructions: two uniformed figures marched to their posts, two uniformed figures marched back to their holes. Repeat. As dawn broke on the ninth day, our sense of security was, however, shattered by the roaring of motors steadily growing stronger as they came closer. We had just enough time to dash out of the house and to the trenches.

Russian tanks steadily rolled towards us followed by armoured vehicles interwoven with Russian infantry yelling their notorious

Urrah! battle cry which sent a chill right to my bones. The defensive barrage ordered by our forward observer was woefully inadequate and barely managed to set the odd vehicle on fire. The heaviest weapons at our disposal in the front trenches were some mortars. Acute shortage in our supplies was one of our most severe obstacles.

'These are about as useful to us as bloody door knockers!' shouted Corporal Huber into my ear. Crouching down next to me he moved his chin towards a box which had only three mortar bombs left. Around us the air was filled by the deafening sounds of explosions, bursts of fire, orders being yelled back and forth and the screaming of injured soldiers. Our MGs rattled incessantly mowing down scores of attacking Russian infantrymen but at the same time their tanks thundered across the trenches, flattening I don't know how many of our men. I would never see Horst, our young recruit, again.

Suddenly Lieutenant Hartmann jumped through the trenches, hopping past one man then another, while keeping blasting short sharp bursts in the direction of the Russians who had come dangerously close.

'Get ready to withdraw!' he kept shouting. 'Take what you can carry! The Reds have penetrated the main battle line – I'm not sure where!'

I had lost sight of him when I checked my ammunition and found, much to my alarm, that I only had five bullets left. Events unfolded swiftly.

Huber grabbed a trench mortar by its barrel while I picked up the box with the three remaining bombs, seeing from the corner of my eye our poacher hoisting the tripod over his shoulder. Pulling ourselves out of the shelter we fell into a backward zigzag run and passing Huber on his right I spotted his broad grin while I, in the meantime, felt nothing but panic and sweat pouring out of my helmet, down my face. Briefly pausing once or twice to catch our breath and get our bearings, we finally reached the far end of the forest. Emerging onto a frost-covered field we met German artillery – some fifty or sixty of them assembled at the forest's edge and gathering in small groups. Wearing a type of camouflage probably made of waterproof tarpaulin with which I wasn't familiar, all were armed with one of the new StG44 assault rifles or had MP 40 sub-machine guns dangling from their necks.

Huber, standing smack in front of me, just mumbled something about them being the SS and that the likes of us could only dream of owning such gear. I could sense his disgust.

Only when the commander of this small unit shouted down from his armoured combat vehicle did my comrade raise his head. Letting the helmet slide to his neck, his expression numb, he barely took in the instructions. 'Your assembly point is straight over there, next to the estate over there – off with you!'

Slowly, staggering rather than walking, we dragged ourselves to the designated spot, more a Polish farm than a German estate. Huber had completely lost his usual good humour, grumbling continuously about our sorry state of equipment. 'If our Jäger were as well-armed as that SS lot over there, we could achieve a hell of a lot more.'

'Goes without saying,' agreed Richard who had all of a sudden and out of nowhere appeared right next to us. 'All I want to know is why this is not the case.'

'Something I've been asking myself all along,' I retorted, while Huber, clearly exasperated, muttered something under his breath.

Hartmann, the sergeant and some others had already gathered in a group and gradually more soldiers trickled in. They were worn out, dispirited and famished. Their faces were grey, their eyes sunk in their sockets. It turned out that ten men were missing.

From that day on, our retreat through Poland moved through various stages. We were much too weak, mentally and physically too depleted and lacking any decent weapons to withstand the over-powering enemy, although we did make several valiant attempts in the way described above. It wasn't just us pioneers, but also the Jäger, the infantry, whose ranks had been utterly decimated during the previous continuous and relentless battles. I certainly wasn't the only one whose once high spirits had given way to utter despondency. But, although we were increasingly discouraged by our unending evacuation and despite our fear of being outstripped, not everyone had given up. 'We mustn't let it come to leaving the doors wide open practically inviting the Russians in,' Richard warned.

'Nobody would want that, Richard. But let me ask you, how on earth and with bloody what are we meant to avert this?'

'Apparently there is talk of some *Wunderwaffen*, some kind of rockets that are meant to be deployed in the next few weeks,' Richard half-hopefully said. 'That's what I overheard the sergeant saying, but I've got no idea whether that's nonsense or invented.'*

'Listen guys,' our 'poacher', having kept himself to himself for quite some time, had once again found his tongue. 'It's going to be Christmas soon, and I for one, though an old fighter, still believe in Father Christmas. But that sure would be one hell of a miracle.'

We laughed, but no one actually felt like it.

We were steadily approaching Poland's western boundary and despite our working tirelessly to lay mines and make use of any and all means available to withstand the onslaught of the Red Army, it seemed to be in vain and the little that was achieved made us feel even more depressed. The land was frozen and it became steadily more difficult to shovel out pits to bury the fallen or trenches to protect those barely standing. The supply of replacement soldiers tapered off. While the pioneers who had recently joined our unit were willing young lads, often even shockingly so, keen to pull the trigger at the drop of a hat, they lacked the training and experience ingrained in the rest of us. Some of them barely survived a day or two.

Then, one morning and much to our amazement, the commander withdrew our unit from the front line. While some feared the worst, others were more keen to believe the rumour that a break was in store for us.

Indeed, that very afternoon trucks brought us to a so-called rest camp. The majority of our sorry lot were in dire need of a break and the moment we had settled onto the cargo platform, we dropped off to sleep, only waking up once we had arrived.

'Finally,' we exclaimed enthusiastically, 'some hot food at long last!' 'Couldn't have come a moment too soon,' remarked Richard and then launched into vivid overstatements of his feelings. 'My

---

* *Wunderwaffen* = wonder weapons. These were promised to the German armed forces and people and would, according to Nazi propaganda, ensure victory.

stomach feels like an empty ice cellar.' We managed something of a smile.

It's astounding what a bit of nourishment and some rest can do for you. We even regained our sense of humour. 'Hey guys, do you miss those shells hailing down on us, as much as I do?'

'Oh, shut up, will you, let's just praise the Lord that it all seems so calm and quiet around here.'

After we wolfed down the steaming hot meat stew that had been ladled out into our mess kits, one of the camp's squad members showed us to a large tent with cots all made up and ready for us. Without letting another second go by I threw myself onto the closest one of these canvas beds and just before drifting into dream world I remember agreeing with comrade Werner Kogler. 'I could definitely stay here for a few weeks,' he sighed contentedly and then he too must have fallen asleep.

The stay was all too brief – we were only given two days, two glorious days of tranquillity in which we could wash both ourselves and our torn and frayed uniforms. We relaxed, ate and slept and were not interrupted once by pointless orders, by the call to go out into the field and lay mines, or the sound of Stuka bombs exploding.

The news which then broke spread like wildfire: the Russians had pushed through our main defences, not once, nor in one spot, but at several points and repeatedly. The imminent threat was that we would be locked in and trapped. Orders were issued thick and fast. Our lot were instructed to disengage immediately and pull further back, dig trenches and plant mines in front of them. Why always us pioneers?

Several trucks had arrived onto which we piled the ammunition and our baggage and then squeezed ourselves into whatever space was available to us. Severely decimated as we were at that time, we actually hardly required more room than we were given. Our vehicles, powered by so-called wood gas – ingeniously invented by engineers back home who had responded to the crippling lack of gasoline – were equipped at their far end with large black cylindrical-shaped metal vessels, some fifty centimetres in diameter, covered with round lids. After one team dumped sacks of chopped wood into these cylindrical boilers, another one would then hermetically seal them, while a flame was ignited via a small door at the bottom of the cylinders sparking a fire that would continue to smoulder and convert the wood to wood gas. This in turn would get pushed through thin metal pipes and power the engine. The entire process was of course hugely laborious and to reach a decent level of power took ages, but it certainly dealt with the short supply of fuel.

I settled down right behind the driver's cabin and next to Richard, leaning myself against one of the sacks filled with wood. 'This area here is at least protected from the winds,' he declared, obviously satisfied with what had come his way.

Most of us seemed focused on the weather.

'Hmmm, it has really turned cold now.'

'Methinks that at least Frau Holle seems to be on strike and hasn't yet granted us any snow, just a bit of frost and ice.'*

'Who cares whether or not there's snow,' one guy interjected impatiently. 'Main thing is that they're not able to encircle us. Become a prisoner of war? That sure is the very last thing I'd wish for.'

In front of us Lieutenant Hartmann led the way in his Kübelwagen which an officer well versed in ground combat had apparently relinquished to him. Once we had crossed the western border of Poland, sooner than anyone expected, we found ourselves on East Prussian territory. All of us fell silent. Briefly my thoughts wandered to the senior sergeant whom I had supported in our mission blowing up the bridge and I could still hear the words he'd said to me at the time. 'If the Russians advance that far, woe betide our wives and children!'

It was somewhere east of Tilsit† that, yet again, we were ordered to dig in. And yet again we did our best to set up home as best we could. I, Corporal Huber, and four others 'lived' in a covered dugout from which we could watch the entire stretch of trenches.

---

* Frau Holle appears in a fairy tale by the Brothers Grimm, who based her on pre-Christian Germanic folklore. The story has it that when she shakes out her pillow, it snows.

† Now Sovetsk, Russia.

By then winter had well and truly set in and it started snowing heavily, covering our lodgings with a thirty- to forty-centimetre-thick layer of snow and making our shelter practically invisible. It wasn't all bad, though. The snow insulated against the cold temperatures outside and also protected us against getting soaked through. We even managed to cobble together some bunk beds out of a few bare tree trunks and before we knew it our dugout had turned into a homely shelter.

But it didn't make a difference to our emotional wellbeing. Despondency, burn-out, fear and cold gnawed on our patience and depleted us of our energy. Thinking himself alone and unobserved I once overheard our youngest comrade staring up at the ceiling, a solid sheet of ice. 'Will we still be around when it starts dripping down from up there?' he murmured out loud, but didn't get a response.

A sense of calm permeated the front; it was as if we were frozen in time, waiting to be woken from our deep winter slumber. We were gripped by the cold, and also by boredom, yet not a single one of us dared venture outside as we were acutely aware of the enemy lying in wait and ready to pounce.

In front of our trenches a narrow river some 15–20 metres wide wound its way eastwards. I forget its name. Embankments free of any trees or shrubbery divided us from the Russians embedded behind the range of hills on the other side. Danger was lurking day and night. But what were we to do? Trying to keep ourselves busy we had shovelled a trench right down to the riverbank, some thirty metres long; we had then camouflaged it and with it now also being concealed under a blanket of snow, it allowed us to fetch water unobserved and at least make some tea for ourselves. Nothing more.

It was Richard's turn to break the silence that had settled upon us. Sitting on a roughly hewn timber bench next to the entrance of our shelter he tried to comfort us. 'I could well imagine staying here for quite a while!' he humoured us.

'Well, I could think of better places to be,' replied Konrad Holzner down from his bunk bed.

Sergeant Huber shouting my name interrupted our brief banter. 'Your turn to go fetch the grub!' he yelled from outside. 'The Hiwi's cart is due to pull in any minute at the meeting point and I don't want you to let the food get cold. I'm famished.'

'We all are!' answered the poacher.

What with the heavy snow clouds low down in the sky it got dark at around 1600. Under cover I made my way along a path which had already been trodden down by the previous food carrier. But I had set out wearing my high rubber boots, in any case, with my feet covered in a pair of wraps which we had been trained to fold correctly around our feet. While they provided some extra warmth, the ferocious cold from the ground penetrated through regardless and I thus quickened my pace. I had decided to leave my coat behind – it was hanging on a hook next to my bunk along with the felt slippers as generally the outside air temperature on that day was relatively mild.

After three minutes I had reached the point at which I was supposed to turn left, cross a small and sparse pine forest and make my way to the *Gulaschkanone*. Just before I got there my comrade Kurt Eisner, who lived in the shelter next to mine, stomped towards me, grumbling something about always being stuck with the same old ghastly grub.

Indeed, watching the Hiwi ladle out some undefined green stuff into the mess kits I had brought along I just pulled a long face. 'Disgusting!' I exclaimed while carefully placing two of the rectangular-shaped mess kits on each of my hands, with a third one precariously balancing atop and crossways over their kidney-shaped covers. Additionally, I also carried tucked under my arms a large bag with a loaf of army bread along with small chunks of cheese. Although that was actually earmarked for breakfast, most of us just gobbled it up straight away. The Hiwi wasn't too insulted by my comments which weren't too complimentary about what I received. 'So long Giorgio!' 'See you soon, Hans!' he shouted after me while I took long strides back to the trench.

Some fifty metres away from where I usually hopped over to our shelter, I could hear a Russian shell detonating right behind my back. Where one shell explodes, more are sure to follow, I thought to myself, and I was well acquainted with their trajectory. First, they travel diagonally upward, then they make a small curve at the top and plunge towards the ground. Hans, I said to myself, you might well be a target. Take full cover, was my instruction to myself; off with you right this minute into the next-best shelter! Much to my annoyance and though falling into the trench just in time, I slid past the latrine and landed way above my ankles in human excrement – luckily half-frozen.

'Shit!' I exclaimed not inappropriately as it turned out, held the food rations high above my head and awkwardly manoeuvred my way over the wooden joist used for sitting. The shell had dug a crater in the ground just a few metres away from me – thank the Lord for small mercies.

The latrine consisted of a short piece of trench, broader and deeper than the normal ones and running parallel to it, so that it could fill up as much as possible before having to be covered by soil, ready for the next layer of faeces. I vented my anger into the silence which had once again fallen all around. 'You damned red assholes over there, couldn't you have sent us your blessings a bit earlier or after supper?'

A little while later I plonked the mess kits and the bread bag on the bench of our bunker.

'Hans, you stink like a sewer!'

'What the hell, did the Hiwi give us shit for our dinner?'

'What the devil did they season our meal with this time?'

'Shut up, you lot!' I yelled incensed. 'If I hadn't jumped in time, you guys would go to bed on an empty stomach, that's for sure, as I would have been a goner along with your grub! Didn't you hear the explosion? Right next to the latrine . . .'

'Of course, Hans, we did hear it, of course!' Huber spoke near-apologetically. 'But we thought you much further away, much further back!' He then handed me a brush. 'You know your way down to the water,' he said with a friendly twinkle in his eyes.

Nodding, but still furious, I grabbed the brush and washed up. When I returned to our 'bunker' with my still wet rubber boots, Richard told me that he was sorry the whole episode was over. 'I'd dearly love to have used the shit to shoot it across to Ivan.'

'I'd rather we do that with our chief of staff!'

Gradually calming down, I devoured my supper although it had got cold in the meantime.

When Huber returned the next day from his meeting with Lieutenant Hartmann we could tell from the furious expression on his face that something was amiss. I couldn't believe my ears when he actually began to speak. 'This big shot above Hartmann must be demented,' Huber blustered, 'he must be bored out of his mind and with nothing to do he came up with an utterly crazy scheme. The front, he claims, is much too calm and we therefore need to take some prisoners, he says, to find out from them what they've got up their sleeve. He then orders me, who, he continues, has such "marvellous men under my command", to send a few of them to infiltrate the enemy and capture two or three Russians. If possible, he added for good measure, we should make sure an officer is among them! And then he continues, sort of coaxing me into his mad idea, telling me that the particular front section under my command is uniquely suitable and that tonight is an especially good time as we're predicted to get heavy clouds and pitch darkness.' And having given his report practically in one breath, Huber looked us straight in the eyes.

'Has he lost his marbles?'

'Probably.'

'He must have shit for brains, this asshole!'

But we realised quickly that the more exasperated we became, the less Huber was likely to take our side. 'We have no choice,' he said calmly, 'but to obey his orders. With our binoculars Hartmann and I have pinpointed the optimal spot to cross the river.' So, we actually had no other option.

'And pray tell us, how are we meant to do this?' Richard wanted to know.

'Silence! I'll tell you straight away as you, my fellow, are part of this excursion,' said Huber, squaring up to Richard. 'We'll be receiving a rubber dinghy but only have permission to inflate it once we reach the exact point from which we are to cross the river – that's some 150 metres away from our water trench. We're of course not able to transport an already pumped-up dinghy through the trench and down to the river. If necessary we'll have to leave it behind when we return. The reason Hartmann and I have chosen that particular location is because there seems to be no, or perhaps only a gentle current.' Then, facing me, he continued. 'You're the third in our party and the poacher back there is the fourth. And now, all of you, pipe down and calm down. Try to snatch a few winks and you'll be good and ready by the evening. Truth be told,' he added in a confidential tone, 'I'm not particularly comfortable with the whole thing, but these are orders.' He sat down.

'A round of *Schafkopf* will do the trick, if you know what I mean. Who can sleep anyway?'* suggested the poacher and with a grin he pulled a pack of playing cards from his back pocket. But Huber put a stop to this straight away. 'No games at this point, only when no one can fall asleep.'

Obediently I stretched out on my bunk and before I knew it, I had fallen into a deep slumber. When I woke up, Huber, the poacher, Richard and Fritz Reich were crouched around our one and only bench playing a round. Fritz got up, passed me his hand saying I should sit in for him while he went to the latrine. 'Don't fall in!' Richard called out to him and, naturally, everyone laughed at the thought.

Before he even returned, two men from the next bunker had already placed the folded dinghy in front of our entrance, along with two paddles and a large hand pump. Throwing us one of those looks which could have indicated either concern or serious reservations about this expedition, they probably were silently thankful that it was us and not them.

'Good luck, the four of you!'

The mission we had been entrusted with had obviously made the rounds. Before departing, one of the guys assured us they had our backs. 'I'm going to be at the MG post. Our guns are in position. The moment you're back on our bank, I'll shower the other side with bullets.'

'Good to know,' retorted our poacher drily. 'Nothing then can happen to us.'

---

* *Schafkopf* is a trick-taking card game popular in Bavaria.

Towards 2200 we silently crawled from the exit of the water trench towards the location from which our crossing was planned to start. The dinghy was pumped up in no time. Richard kneeled at the far end; I was at the top end. In front of us some fifteen metres of black water and though the night wasn't as pitch dark as anticipated due to the snow being so bright, we could hardly make out the other side of the river. We had agreed that we'd row the dinghy across by applying long, vigorous but soft paddle strokes. The rest of our crew huddled low. Once ashore, we heard some loud rustling so we kept still for a few minutes intensely straining our ears to pick up where the noise was coming from.

'Up there, behind the bushes, there must be a guard post,' I could hear Huber whispering.

'Our lot have been firing from time to time for several hours, so that these guys don't get wind of us.'

'Go!' I heard Huber whisper and with that the three silhouettes, each armed with nothing but a pistol, were off, just above my head, and vanished into the dark. I was tasked to watch the boat and was equipped with a handful of egg grenades. It's hard to capture what I was feeling back then, alone in the dark. Despite the regular periods of gunfire delivered by our squad back on the other side, I thought after about half a minute that I could clearly make out the distinct sound of pistol shots coming from the direction in which the other three had disappeared.

A quarter of an hour later I knew that the Russian guard must have been killed before being able to raise the alarm. My three comrades returned with two Russians, one ordinary soldier and one sergeant. The two held their hands above their heads but refused to get on board the boat. But with the muzzles of Huber's and Richard's Lugers thrust into their back, they could be convinced that all resistance was going to come to nought.

Sliding our oars into the water with full force, no longer at pains to avoid making noise, I hissed softly across to Huber: 'How was it?' 'Later . . . we're not done yet,' he said, still concentrating.

We landed safely but in the meantime there were signs that the Russians behind and above us had woken up. They must have discovered the two dead bodies. Huber and the poacher shoved the prisoners towards our water trench, while Richard and I quickly kicked the boat back into the river, flung the paddles into the water and sank the air pump.

The mission overall had only lasted some twenty minutes but had put us under such tremendous stress that once it was all over we felt huge relief. A huge burden had been lifted from our shoulders.

I was the last one into the trench, but managed to overhear Huber deliver his report to our lieutenant who stood next to the MG post. 'We ambushed two soldiers and one officer in their dugout – they were busy cleaning their rifles. The officer was about to raise the alarm. I smashed my Luger into his face, but had to finish him off with a bullet to his head. He just refused to remain calm and would have given us away! We wouldn't have had a chance in hell.'

And at that very moment the Russians began to pound our MG positions, firing indiscriminately with explosions echoing far across the landscape but causing limited damage.

Hartmann had to shout over the cacophony of gunfire howling and blasting through the air to make himself heard: 'That was to be expected! Thankfully they only woke up once it was too late for them! Don't worry yourself, Huber,' he added, hoping to reassure him. 'Our good sergeant-major can't really expect us to serve him up an entire Russian army corps, for God's sake, he'll just have to make do with those two guys.' With that he followed his privates who were pushing the two prisoners along the trench, but not before turning around to give Huber praise. 'You've done well, Huber,' he shouted. 'Get back to your wigwam now, there's a bottle of cognac and four packs of cigarettes for your guys – you've sure earned them!'

'Thank you, lieutenant!'

The storm of gunfire slowly died down and with it our stress level of the past hour, making room for a huge sense of satisfaction. The alcohol certainly had the desired impact on us, most certainly on myself. But what I enjoyed above all and to the fullest were my Eckstein cigarettes which the likes of us Landsers rarely got to see.

Towards seven in the morning, while it was still dark, Huber was ordered to the rear bunker to report to Hartmann. On his return we looked at him expectantly, but were somewhat let down by what Huber relayed. 'Yup,' he said, 'report was made. Sergeant-major was also present. He complained, I've got to admit, about this and that. Mind you, he had some words of praise for our courage and the successful outcome of our mission but was displeased that we hadn't brought with us the map pouch of the Russian officer. He was of the opinion that this pouch would most definitely have contained more information than the two squirts we'd brought had to divulge. And on top of it all, the sergeant-major was annoyed about the fact that we'd now lost the element of surprise which we had going for ourselves! But yes, he was proud of us and glad that I and you guys had returned safely.' That was not all. Huber then relayed his part of the conversation and how he tried to justify what we had or hadn't done. '"Sergeant-major, sir," I told him, "We frankly didn't have the time to search the guy for his pouch. The Russians, we feared, could wake up at any moment and either make mincemeat of us or take us prisoners."' According to Huber the sergeant-major apparently agreed, but nevertheless regretted that we had blown an opportunity.

'Bloody difficult man to please, this sergeant-major.' Richard was quite agitated. 'But don't fret, Huber!' he appeased our boss. 'You're not going to bump into him very soon, seeing that this fine gentleman wouldn't be caught dead sleeping out here in the front trench.'

The next day we were informed that there was a breakfast delivery due and once again it fell upon my good self to fetch it for our six men. Stepping out from our bunker, I literally couldn't believe my eyes. The misty grey weather had quite literally dampened our mood during the past weeks or so, but on that day I was greeted by a crystal-clear blue sky with the sun smiling down from above. Not a single cloud to be seen.

'Now what's that all about,' I mumbled to myself half-smiling. 'Are we in for spring?' Softly I began to whistle a merry tune.

'Well, how about that, private Beanpole! You sure look like you're enjoying this unexpected spring weather!' said Max Pfeifer from his well-camouflaged MG post, himself in obviously good spirits as well. I spent a few minutes chatting to him, briefly forgetting how much taller than him I was and that my head must have peeked out from above the edge of the trench. Suddenly I heard something hissing past my left ear and sensed immediate and burning pain – as if stung by a glowing needle.

'For goodness sake, Hans, of course the Russian snipers on the other side would take such fine weather to exercise their sharp-shooting skills!' exclaimed Max with a mixture of reproach and dismay.

He shut up when he saw me kneeling on the ground trying to stop the blood dripping down my neck with the help of the bandages I always kept on me.

'Hold on, Hans, I'll help you.'

We finally managed, not without difficulty, to dress the wound which the grazing shot had caused with Max still trying to cheer me up. 'Hard to believe that there's so much juice in your ear lobe,' he commented. 'You've been very lucky, old fellow, three or four centimetres further left and you'd be on your way to meet your maker. I realised too late that you were being quite foolhardy.'

I could only nod, then slowly got up, dragged myself through the camouflaged entrance and onwards to the waiting *Gulaschkanone*.

The gloriously sunny day only lasted until that evening and once again a blanket of thick clouds and fog descended on the landscape. At some point during that time Huber had rejoined us from the rear area where he must have had a meeting with Hartmann. 'The sergeant has actually put us four up for the Iron Cross Second Class and has apparently also suggested that we receive the Close Combat Clasp seeing as we've seen the enemy eye-to-eye more often than is strictly required in order to qualify.' He relayed all this somewhat derisively.

We had much the same couldn't-care-less reaction as Huber did. Nobody could have predicted at the time, however, that Hartmann's application on our behalf would get lost amidst all the mayhem that was breaking out.

In the meantime, I was promoted to lance-corporal. I was still only seventeen years old, and though still young I realised that I was no longer filled with my erstwhile confidence in our victory nor with the enthusiastic fighting spirit I once was so proud of. Instead, all I felt was disenchantment and frustration. Ever since being deployed at the front we had experienced nothing but defeat. None of us simple soldiers could miss the tell-tale signs of the growing gaps in our ranks and the general sense that we, once strong and mighty, were now weak. Of those who had marched to Ingolstadt station accompanied by military music, many had been killed – and a large number of those clueless young lads who had only joined us more recently hadn't lasted for more than a day or two. It was only the deep-seated sense of obedience which had been drilled into us over the years that kept me going, as well as an embedded sense of duty to defend our homeland against the Russians.

My comrades thought and felt much along the same lines, yet nobody dared voice their opinions freely. This, of course, would have been tantamount to undermining the military forces, punishable, as we would hear by word of mouth, by death by hanging or a firing squad, though thankfully nothing of the sort had ever taken place in our company. Others, accused of cowardice before the enemy, were condemned to death. It took less than a minute for the sentence to be issued.

The terrain in the narrow strip of the front line which we occupied was less than ideal for tanks and heavy vehicles and though we were just about able to defend ourselves against the onslaughts of the enemy infantry, news that the Russians had now also broken through our positions in the south had us sink further into depression.

'The danger is real – we're about to be encircled.'

'Being taken POW by the Russians? I can't bear the thought . . . just hope our mates will get us out of here!' Such and similar rumours buzzed through the trenches while it slowly began dawning on me that we hadn't laid eyes on an officer for days.

'There's no way we can allow the Russians to penetrate further into our land.'

'Absolutely right –we can't let it come to that.'

Once again, I asked myself why it was that time and time again us little folks were left to wonder, left in uncertainty and fear. Why weren't we being told what was going on for real? Why was it that all we were good for was to be given orders?

It was one evening in late November, or perhaps early December 1944, that we got the order to retreat. Most of us set about packing our belongings in silence, then got ourselves to the baggage trucks to help with loading. Huber, Richard, our poacher and myself were instructed to remain behind as the rearguard and were ordered to let off short bursts of gunfire occasionally to lull our enemy into believing that we had a carefully orchestrated defence.

'But if they attack us at dawn, we're screwed,' mumbled Richard for just myself to hear.

'Idiot – by then we are off and far away.'

'Aha, smartie pants, sure … if it continues like that our final victory is just around the corner!'

'Shut up, will you!'

The dense clouds above us were lifting and our eyes were fixed on the hazy landscape spreading far in front of our trenches. Towards 2200 a messenger jumped into our section. 'Depart! We're off.'

Richard shouldered his MG, I slung the gun mount and my felt shoes across my shoulders and we were gone. Nothing was left behind except for a few tread mines for the Russians to step on. 'Let that be our welcoming gift for the new inhabitants of our wigwam,' Huber commented sarcastically.

Without making a sound we scurried through the night. The trucks were waiting for us at the rear, fitted with wood burners of course. We mounted the last one and were off. The cloud cover above us thinned and eventually allowed a bright moon to shine down on us. It was a crisp and dry night.

This time round I was seated next to Huber, atop a box of unknown contents, staring out across the dusky countryside. I could eventually make out the contours of dark pine forests bordering the many lakes we travelled past, some smaller, some larger, while I discovered that the trees lining the alleyway we rumbled along were all majestic oaks probably hundreds of years old.

'There are supposed to be hills around here, reaching some 300 metres high!' someone shouted.

'That's quite right,' agreed Huber, and I yet again marvelled at his vast knowledge, this time concerning Masuria and its 3,000 lakes.

He proceeded to expound on the beauties of this enchanting region, enthusiastically sharing tit-bits about the natural beauties of the Spirding, the Löwentin and the Mauersee.*

'Have you actually visited these places before?' Richard was curious to find out.

'Yes, before the war. My aunt was married to a man employed on one of these grand country estates. You wouldn't believe how breath-taking it is around here in the summer.'

'Breath-taking?' growled the poacher. 'You can say that again. But it's air poisoned with lead that's taking our breath away these days, what with the war still raging.'

We must have been driving for some three or four hours when we arrived at several very well equipped positions occupied by our infantry. Stopping right in front of some tents which had been prepared for us, we dismounted from our trucks, totally stiff and frozen to the bone. Once again comments and rumours abounded. 'Looks like we're in for a treat . . . even at this late stage of the game.'

'Believe it or not, we are now posted *behind* the infantry! Usually it's the other way round.'

'Pretty incredible!' someone else added. 'Are we really to thank our major for putting all this in place for us?'

'Can't believe it myself. Has mister sergeant-major suddenly discovered that his heart is beating? That he's got feelings for his men?'

'I admit . . . myself I'm not so sure about this,' another one inter-jected. 'My guess is that mister sergeant-major wants to keep us sweet so that we lay mines around the border of the lake.'

'Haven't you noticed? The lake is well covered by a sheet of ice. My guess is that in this freezing weather the thickness will be such that it will allow vehicles to cross. So, here's what I am hoping for: let us for heaven's sake not be ordered to lay the mines across the ice!'

'Idiot! Can you imagine the fantastic targets we'd become? We'd be mowed down.'

---

* Respectively Sniardwy, Niegocin and Mamry, in Poland's Masurian Lakes district.

'Agreed. And, as usual, in front of the infantry.'

'What's the name of this lake, anyway?'

'No idea, but someone told me that a town called Lötzen[*] borders the northern shore of this lake where the front has been adjusted – the Russians have already pushed through to the east of us and are embedded somewhere on the shore opposite.'

With these thoughts still jumbling in my head I went into the tent, which was moderately warmed up by a small, round iron stove, but was quite amazed to see to the right and left of a narrow corridor ten camp beds each lined up with tarpaulin mattresses and neatly covered by folded blankets.

'Sure haven't been welcomed to such smart lodgings in quite a while,' I spontaneously remarked.

'I'm with you, sure, but can't help wondering, where's the catch?' Richard was not one to be fooled.

And indeed, a loud voice from the back of the tent would prove his suspicions right. 'Huber has been given the order to make regular checks of the ice thickness and report the results to the rear by telephone. I'm pretty sure this means that we'll have to lay mines into the frozen lake.

This piece of news was followed by a long period of silence. Everyone was sunk in thoughts. I was no exception in fearing that this could only bode ill.

But then, once we reported on day two or three to Huber that the ice sheet was indeed thick and sturdy enough to bear even heavier vehicles, we were well surprised to watch how horse-driven carts loaded with manure drove out towards the middle of the lake and began lining up to form one long barricade. Nobody bothered to find out from where these horse carriages and their freight actually came.

The Russians, on the other hand, certainly became aware of the unusual activity on the large ice expanse and relentlessly swept the entire area with gunfire, bullets ploughing into the ice cover, but causing little damage other than some dark shimmering holes

---

[*] Now Giżycko, Poland.

gleaming out of the lake. We could only be thankful that the shore occupied by the Russians was a fair distance away from us.

Without saying a word, we stood on the embankment, staring out into the night. It was obvious to us that this would be our task from then on, night after night: moving the mine belt, row after row after row. And each one of us knew how to go about it. We'd take an ice-pick, bore small holes into the ice in which we would place the bottle mines and activate them. Thank goodness for the long distance between us and the Russians on the other side of the lake, we thought, as they wouldn't be able to hear us. Any niggling fears or better judgement we still had, didn't keep us from muttering expletives and making snide remarks.

'Mister sergeant-major apparently is of the opinion that dung produces heat and the ice will therefore melt.'

'What a joke! The guy knows zilch about farming.'

'But there definitely is an advantage to this dung being heaped up on the lake. Once the barricade is frozen it will definitely provide us with some protection when the Russians decide to blast their bullets across the lake.'

'Sure is comforting what you're telling us here. I feel much better already.'

'Well, I don't. If the Russians advance from where they're positioned now, they'll be able to launch their shells at us without any hindrance . . . we'll be turned into sieves – there's no two ways about it.'

'Oh come on you lot, why shit in your pants.' Huber sounded as calm and collected as if we were sitting safely back in the trench.

The very next night we were ordered to drive mines into the ice sheet at a distance of some hundred metres from the wide dung barricade that had, as predicted, hardened to a rock-solid fortification. As per usual I was labouring away alongside Huber, Richard and the poacher. The others too were old hands at this job. A sharp, icy wind was whistling about our ears, blasting ice crystals into our faces making them burn as if we'd been stung by a hundred needle pricks. It wasn't possible to wear our gloves throughout, as the different steps we needed to perform required using our bare hands.

Numb with cold, we desperately tried rubbing them together but it didn't do much for us. The stormy wind had, however, the advantage that it blocked out all the sound which was unavoidably caused by grinding into the ice to make the holes.

Us four were saddled with what must have been at least three shifts that night, tirelessly shoving reinforced supplies of mines from the storage place to the shore. Yet this too had something going for it as the constant lugging and transporting got our blood circulation going with eventually our fingertips regaining their feeling – a painful sensation. Had we not worn the felt boots which we had organised for ourselves we would most certainly have suffered frostbite and even loss of our feet.

We slaved away for some four nights, working like crazy without a single break with the result that our mine belt extended way beyond the wall of dung.

It was rumoured that even our sergeant-major had words of praise for our efforts, probably not least because the explosives we were burying in the ice were named after him – apparently he had invented them. These consisted of small wooden boxes filled with dynamite and fitted with a pedal, which, once pushed down, would blow off an enemy's leg without, however, killing him.

'Small mercies,' growled Huber while we were busy sinking the first of those explosives into the ice.

Christmas Eve was no different and once again we were ordered out onto the lake. The large surface, in the meantime covered by a thirty-centimetre-thick snow layer, appeared eerily lit and despite the darkness of the night and a clouded sky overhanging the countryside we could make out the shadowy contours of the landscape surrounding us. On some level I was reminded of the Bodensee and, turning to Richard who was walking next to me, I asked whether he knew the ballad of the *Reiter vom Bodensee*.*

'Sure thing, I didn't play truant my entire time at school, you know. But seems to me the Russians are made of tougher stuff than our horseman.'

---

* '*Die Ballade des Reiters vom Bodensee*' ('The Ballad of the Horseman of Lake Constance') tells the story of a rider crossing a frozen lake.

In order not to draw too much attention to ourselves while we were working, seeing as the lake literally served us up as if on a silver platter, we wore white camouflage over our uniforms. It had been impressed upon each and every one of us to be particularly alert and attentive on that night, as the Russians were well aware that the Germans liked to indulge in celebrations on that date. We fully expected the enemy to launch an attack, but the command post gave us permission to withdraw to our tents towards 2300.

On our way back we passed several infantry guards on duty who kindly invited us into their shelters and trenches to share with them a warm drink. My guess was that none of these foot soldiers were much older than us yet their faces were drawn, haggard and marked by war as if they were our seniors. On that evening especially, under the sparse candle-light flickering from the thin little Christmas trees and opening their letters from loved ones at home, profound longing stared out of their eyes. A deep sense of sadness pervaded all of us.

While it was much warmer than outside down in the trenches of the infantry, cosy even, we didn't want to linger as we also were hoping that some mail would be waiting for us back in our tents, maybe even a parcel or two.

As I was the last one to leave, a corporal grabbed me by my sleeves trying to get my attention. He wanted to get more information as they obviously knew we had been up closest to the enemy. 'You've been able to see more out there than us stuck here. D'you think the Russians will leave us be today?'

Richard had overheard the question and responded in my stead. 'You know yourself that these guys are unpredictable. Maybe they'll save their ammo for another day, maybe not. Be on your guard!'

On that Christmas night we were indeed able to sleep for several hours uninterrupted, without being woken either by orders or enemy fire. But this did nothing to lift our mood or to take us away from our thoughts about our families at home, our life and celebrations lying far back in the past. As for me, I was in particular discomfort as my lower belly was badly hurting especially when urinating. That night, the pain was more excruciating than it had been during the previous three days and nights I had laboured through, out on the ice.

My situation didn't go unnoticed and the following day Huber approached me. 'Hans,' he said, quite concerned, 'I've been watching you for a while and you simply can't continue this way. You're to head back right this minute and report to Hartmann. Up to him what should happen with you.'

A quarter of an hour later I was handed my marching orders, signed by the chief of our company, and instructed to travel to the field hospital in Allenstein.* 'Fackler, nobody needs to tell me that you're a good soldier. But you also need to be a healthy one. Now, get yourself off to hospital, make sure you return to us soon. I want to see you fit and in fighting spirit.' He paused and then remarked more to himself than to me that he had actually been expecting many more casualties considering the freezing temperatures out there on the ice. 'In fact, sergeant-major has now ordered three days' downtime; it's rest and refit for our lot and then get ready for renewed action.'

Standing erect in front of him I didn't say anything. 'You know where to get the train. It's out of range of their artillery, so off you go.'

Once again I found myself on the horse cart and driving with the Hiwi the short distance to the designated stop, with the constant artillery fire well within earshot. We had grown accustomed to it. Only when the shells fell nearer to us did we draw in our heads and listen intently; when the blasts that followed felt too close for comfort we jumped down from the narrow bench of the vehicle. But then on it went with our small shaggy Russian horse pulling us along.

The Hiwi wouldn't take me the whole way, so I continued for some two hours on foot arriving just a few minutes before the train departed. I wasn't the only injured soldier on this journey. In my compartment alone there were several men with blood-soaked dressings covering their faces and barely bandaged wounds on their arms and legs. None of us spoke, we just silently stared out of the window into the East Prussian countryside overhung by heavy grey clouds which sharp wind storms were blowing eastward. After a change-over in Ortelsburg† I arrived in Allenstein at 1400.

---

* Now Olsztyn, Poland.

† Szczytno, Poland.

The field hospital, housed temporarily in what had previously served as a school building, was a busy scene of nurses and camp aides rushing around not much bothered by the newcomers. The doctor, a young man wearing a blood-stained white coat, briskly examined and rather curtly dismissed my condition. 'Oh, for goodness' sake, this certainly isn't anything serious. Nothing but a urinary tract infection caused by the cold. I'd say there's plenty worse around here. I'm giving you an injection and then off with you immediately! Back to the front, where you belong.'

I'm not quite sure what this young medic shot up my veins, but I definitely felt quite dizzy afterwards. However, I have to admit it worked. Towards 1800 I was back on the train, and though by now surrounded by darkness, I could make out that only old sweats were in the wagon – mainly guys who had lost touch with their units and now were plucked out from field hospitals and convalescent camps to be pushed to the front once again. Glancing around in the dim light, all I could see was a collection of haggard faces with despondency staring out of their eyes and I had to muster all my energy not to let myself be affected by the gloomy situation.

Once we had pulled into Ortelsburg it was announced that the next train would only depart at 0300, so in the middle of the night the prospect of some wonderful spare time coming my way was ahead of me. Since I felt hardly any pain at all, just a bit of drowsiness, I made my way to the mess, which basically was a well-heated foyer for soldiers. The hot tea poured into my mess kit warmed my insides and the few slices of army bread spread with artificial honey tasted like a delicacy.

It was pitch dark when I descended from the train, which had come to a stop on a wide-open field, supposedly close to my destination. I had a hard time orientating myself, but eventually found my way back to my comrades.

While in Allenstein all I could hear was a dull noise of the artillery at work; around here the bangs of crackling gunshots sounded sharper and the explosions more thunderous with each kilometre I put behind me – the everyday story of life at the front. Twice or three times I was forced to take full cover, throwing myself down as the whistling of the shell gave me the tell-tale tip-off that it would soon hit the ground just near me. Once again the front owned me body and soul. While ducking and dodging, weaving my way forward, I couldn't quite explain why, but I felt that where I belonged was here at the front, together with my comrades, and that without them I'd actually feel lost.

I got there round about when the first ray of daylight pierced through the grey clouds and a light snow flurry drizzled down. The minute I arrived I was surrounded by voices I recognised while numerous hands thumped my back in welcome. 'Good, you've arrived just in time!'

'Better believe it, another half-an-hour and we'd be gone.'

'The Russians have made another breakthrough.'

'The infantry cleared out a while ago. But we had to stay behind and help with lugging the equipment onto the vehicles.'

'Hartmann has already left.'

'Hans, rumour has it that we're being moved to the area around Königsberg.* All hell has broken loose there, we're told.'

I climbed up onto the loading area of the truck carrying our baggage and joined Richard sitting on a carton labelled 'trench mines'.

'We've come up in the world,' he commented sarcastically. 'Look, this time it's diesel power for us.'

'The Russians haven't yet got wind that we're departing,' thought our 'poacher' who sat with Huber on a similar carton next to us.

'What makes you think that?' asked a thin voice belonging to one of the now steadily diminishing number of reinforcement soldiers.

'Clear as rain, little guy. Don't you realise they're still targeting the positions way behind us . . . ?'

'Oh shut up, poacher, will you! The boy will wise up soon enough, if he lives that long.' Huber sounded calm as usual.

'How many are we, actually?' I asked him.

'Don't know myself, to be honest. Yesterday "cobbler" got a splinter dug into his shoulder and grocer Heinrich got caught in his leg. Both

---

* Now Kaliningrad, Russia.

are being repaired by the sweet nurses in Allenstein. My guess is that with you included we've probably reached thirty-two again.'

A thick cover of snow enveloped us. Later that afternoon we suddenly received the order to dismount while the vehicles with our stuff, equipment and mines rolled on.

'Listen up, everyone!' shouted Sergeant Moser. 'This place here is called Neuhausen* and is a suburb of Königsberg. A factory of military importance used to be here and what we have in front of us,' he explained with an expansive hand movement, 'is this desolate field right up to the forest, which was or still is a landing strip for aircraft. As you can see, there's no longer anybody around.' Indeed, following the direction of his hand, all we could see was a huge empty plot. 'We've been ordered to remain here, play the forward post so to speak, and wait for our next orders,' he continued. 'We've got plenty of hand grenades, plenty of ammunition – just no food. I hope we'll find something edible in these farms scattered around here and then we'll set up home.'

'But where are the Russians hiding?' someone wanted to know. 'For you to find out!' answered someone else.

'Silence!' yelled Moser, clearly furious. 'The T-34s don't operate at night. But the Russians can always be relied on for coming up with a surprise. So, with a relief every two hours, I want double sentries just next to the shed in front of the runway, direction east. Above all, keep your eyes on this area bordering the forest. As for the area round about, I'm immediately putting double patrols together. Dismissed!'

Discipline had unravelled and our group was milling around, long having done away with the strict line-up of previous months. Slowly, reluctantly, everyone gradually dispersed. Richard and I were on the first sentry duty and posted ourselves in front of the long barn as ordered. Somehow, we had both expected to find an abandoned aircraft hangar but once inside the sight took our breath away. Never before had we seen so many rare and beautiful horses as we did on that day – chained along the right- and left-hand side, barely moving, they stood in front of their crated mangers and empty feeding troughs. We counted twenty animals. Their narrow, light-

---

* Guryevsk, Russia.

brown faces turned towards us, some were neighing softly, others nibbled hungrily at the straw from their litter. A scandal!

The stalls at the rear were empty. Obviously, the people had just buggered off in their horse carriages, as there were none around. 'My bet is that the Russians are much closer than they want us to believe,' muttered Richard, for once sounding unusually agitated. 'I'll go to Huber and ask if Sepp and Fritz can help us out here. Both are farmer's sons and they'll know how to feed and water these poor animals.'

'Go ahead!' I shouted over my shoulder while walking down the centre aisle of the horse stable which was pleasantly warm. Carefully I opened the sliding gate just enough to look outside and onto the large snow-covered stretch of land which had been described to us as the runway. All was still, as far as I could see, when suddenly I heard a soft whimpering from a bay that was separated from the rest of the stalls by a wooden screen. Might there be some more horses around, I asked myself and stepped inside.

A robust workhorse stood there chained to the wall amid a large piled-up heap of straw with its plump buttocks towards me. Staring at me with its large eyes, it neighed quietly as if asking me to feed and water it. Only then did I notice that its iron feeding tray was empty, but that there was a water tap next to its stall on the side wall. Underneath stood an overturned bucket. Without wasting any more time, I simply filled it with water, poured it swiftly into the stone trough and while the animal lapped it up greedily, I was already busy filling the bucket a second time.

Outside the enclosure, the stable had returned to life and I heard Sepp calling excitedly that he had made a find. 'In the shed right next door there's everything we need for the horses! I haven't ever seen such beautiful long-legged creatures at home, ever,' he enthused. 'By the way and to let you know, "poacher" and the others in the farmhouse are busy cooking up a storm for us all. We'll never be able to put it all away, I can bet you! A full stomach for us, finally!'

'That's welcome news, indeed,' I heard Fritz reply. 'It's about time something came our way, and we'd better get to it before the Russians do.'

'Oh, stop it Fritz, why do you always have to paint the devil on the wind – quite literally I mean?' grumbled Sepp.

Not really paying attention to much of the chatter, I patted the horse on its neck, stroked its nostrils as gently as I could and was happy when it snorted trustingly in response. Only then did my eyes fall onto a full pile of clean straw stacked up behind the boxes of the horses. Calling across to the other two to help themselves to it, I had, in the meantime, formed an idea. 'Don't forget to feed the gelding,' I told them. 'I've already given it some water. And tonight I'll be sleeping here in the straw. It's warm at least!'

'Fine, Hans. If you're slated for guard duty, we'll know where to find you.'

On stepping into the spacious kitchen of the farmhouse some two hours later, I suddenly felt my stomach cramp up and it only hit me then how famished I was. The sight I beheld while still glued to the threshold was too good to be true, but there it was: a long table laden with masses of food – and all set with plates and cutlery! With Heinz Weber, Schorsch Meindl and the poacher standing around the burning stove, blue aprons tied around their waists and their contented faces flushed by the steam, it was like in a picture book. The whole room felt cosy and warm.

'Where the hell did you manage to pick up all of that and what's sizzling over there?' I asked nodding towards the stove.

'Moser thought we were the best cooks among our lot and put us in charge. We're having roast pork, potato dumplings and fresh cabbage salad.'

Some comrades, so ran the story, had found a recently slaughtered pig in a neighbouring farm. Musing about the words 'recently slaughtered' and putting two and two together, I was quite sure that the people who had lived there had fled in a panic.

Six men, already sitting pretty at the table with expectant looks on their faces like children waiting for their Christmas presents, were ready to dig in. One of them, by the name of Emil Gschwandt, shouted across to me without taking his eyes away from the plate: 'Hans, you and I are on patrol duty, so you'll be eating with the first lot and then after patrol it'll be your turn to take a nap.'

We enjoyed a delicious meal which of course got tongues wagging again.

'There are no horses on any of the other estates. My guess is that the inhabitants have fled using their coaches,' reported someone.

'So much then for the *Endsieg*, comrades,'* stated Emil, not even trying to hide his sarcasm, upon which Huber threw him a disapproving look.

'Emil, you better stop thinking out loud. That can be dangerous for you should the wrong guy happen to overhear it.'

'No wrong guys around here.'

And so it went on without anyone's appetite in the least bit spoilt.

Between 2000 and 2200 Emil and I, equipped with our felt boots, stomped through the freshly fallen snow hardly making a sound. With the silence of the dark and empty houses around us and nothing moving in the fields, the landscape appeared ghostly. 'What might be holding up the Russians?' asked Emil in a whisper. 'Why on earth would they be any slower than us. D'you think they're taking the piss out of us?'

'But surely you know that they never or hardly ever use their T-34s at night?'

'Sure, I know that, but what about their infantry? They've got as many men as there are grains of sand on the beach.'

'Well that's just it,' said Huber appearing from behind the corner of a house. 'Moser ordered me to check on you, by the way.' Again he seemed unusually irritated. 'He's too lazy to do this himself and is lying all comfy in his bed over at the farm – mind you in full uniform and his gun at the ready. He doesn't much trust this calm either. So, keep your eyes and ears open! Mark my words, this is just temporary, a breather . . . there's definitely no relying on it. See you later.'

After our replacements had arrived, I chatted a bit with them while they took up their posts at the entrance to the stable. Noting a pair of binoculars hanging from the poacher's neck I wondered where he

---

* *Endsieg* = final victory, an expression describing Nazi Germany's supposedly coming triumph.

could possibly have kept them during the past weeks. 'Where did you get those from?'

'Over there in the villa,' he answered, well pleased with himself. 'I sort of stumbled across a beautifully carved gun cabinet – but other than these,' he said, lifting the binoculars into the air, 'it was empty. Why don't you have a turn with them. The sharpness is so incredible: even with this hazy moonlight you'll be able to see each and every small branch of the trees at the edge of the forest!' He was about to slip them over his head to hand them to me.

'Sure, I'd love to, but I'm so exhausted now that all I want to do is join my horse over in the barn and throw myself onto the pile of straw. Good luck, you two!'

Content, still on a full stomach, I stretched out in the straw and was out like a light. I don't know how long I was asleep, dead to the world, but suddenly was woken up by hooves clip-clopping on the stable's cobble-stoned floor. Just about to get up, I could feel my four-legged friend rubbing his moist muzzle against my head. Somehow the horse had managed to undo its chain and there it stood, towering over me, erect to its full height and with its strong front legs like pillars smack in front of my face.

The next rota had, in the meantime, taken up their guard positions and they too had heard the clippety-clops of the hooves. Inside, Heiner Drexler wanted to know whether the bulldog, as he decided to call the horse, had wanted to trample me. But Heinz Weber, his comrade and son of a farmer with an estate somewhere in the Alpenvorland, set him straight. 'Dummy! No horse would do such a thing. What you don't know is that if horses behave this way, they may appear aggressive but in truth they really aren't. I've got that from my father. Apparently, it's totally the opposite when it comes to women.'

'And what would you know about women!'

'Hans,' insisted Heiner, 'do me a favour and put the chain back on this animal. Better safe than sorry.'

I was actually quite surprised at how willingly the gelding followed me once I got hold of his mane to lead him back to his stall where he made no difficulties when I chained him to the beam.

After a rushed cat's lick under the tap, which obviously only ran cold water, I went back to sleep, losing myself in a dream where I watched horses galloping through meadows and fields through a hilly landscape that was pleasantly broken up by lakes of crystal blue.

The following day went by without anything particularly note-worthy happening. Just shortly before lunch I could see Hartmann standing with Sergeant Moser deep in conversation, but couldn't catch what it was they were saying. Our poacher standing next to me offered me a cigarette from a newly opened pack. 'And where d'you have these from, might I ask?'

'Oh, these were in a desk drawer in that noble mansion I told you about, where I found the binoculars,' he said nonchalantly. 'I might actually take myself over there in just a moment . . . perhaps I'll find more useful stuff.'

'Seems like we're left to look after ourselves these days,' I mused.

'Yes, quite. But while it was manageable before, it's a different story ever since supplies failed to materialise and no reinforcement is forthcoming . . . Yup, that's exactly how I had imagined our *Endsieg* . . .'

Seriously worried about the uncertain future which seemed in store for us, conflicted about what I was, or should be, hoping for, I was confused. Was there going to be an *Endsieg*? Could we believe in the promises of the *Wunderwaffen*, or was it all hollow words, meaningless propaganda? It all seemed a muddle and so I just concentrated on blowing the perfect smoke rings into the clear winter air. Doubts like these had been plaguing me for a while.

After our plentiful lunch, Huber, in his usual composed manner, made an announcement and while its content startled us, it at long last pulled us out of our limbo. 'Tomorrow morning four Tiger tanks are scheduled to arrive,' he informed us as if it was the most obvious development to expect. 'Over there,' he lifted his head in the direction of the forest, 'we'll see some life returning. I'm not exactly sure who spilled the beans to our top guns, and why we're only being told now, but there it is.' He obviously didn't want any questions. 'We ourselves haven't noticed anything which would have alerted us to this; but we've got to keep reminding ourselves about one thing and one thing only: it will not remain as peaceful as we've had it for the past few days. Eyes and ears are to be kept open, we mustn't be taken unawares and must not tolerate any sudden visitor – certainly not before those tanks which are meant to protect us have arrived!'

'Never have I clapped my eyes on any of those so-called wonderful tanks!' announced Richard for everyone to hear.

'Look at that! Come to think of it, nor have I,' responded another. 'And that's me who's been part of the withdrawal of the front line for absolute ages.'

'But these tanks really should do the job,' opined yet another. 'Apparently the Russian ones can't hold a candle to them.'

'You might be right in this regard, but they have more of them . . . and that holds true for the infantry as well – they literally have millions. Surely you didn't miss that one?'

This sparring match lasted for quite a while until finally Huber put a stop to it. 'Get out of here! All of you! The next shift also wants to get to eat.'

Tense and yet full of expectation we eagerly waited for the next morning to break. And because my birthday falls on 21 January, I know that it was two days later, on 23 January that, lo and behold, four Tigers rumbled through the parish that we occupied, eventually coming to a screeching halt in front of our lodgings. Jumping down from the turret of the first tank, the commander, with his Iron Cross clearly visible, yelled towards our group, which had just barely managed to gather into some kind of formation, that under no circumstances was any time to be wasted. 'It's crucial that the Russians must be taken by surprise. We'll now turn the corner round this house, move into their vision, and the four of us will then align one next to the other at a distance fifty metres apart. You will support the attack. Stay behind us at all times, in four groups, eight men each.' Glancing to our sergeant he wanted to double-check that. 'Thirty-two men, correct?'

'Yes, sir!'

'Good. Follow us and you'll be well protected. Only the Russian infantry could become a problem. If they do, we'll give you a hand with our MGs! Let's go!'

It wasn't pure coincidence that I together with Huber and six others were standing right behind this commander who was so brimming with confidence, and his decisiveness certainly rubbed off on us. We couldn't wait to launch ourselves into what appeared to us to be a new phase of the war.

'The other tank commanders are officers as well and have a great deal of front experience,' one guy in our group claimed to know.

'The T-34s don't have a chance in hell against our anti-tank weapons, just you wait and see!'

'They're unbelievably expensive, I have it on good authority, so they must be deployed sparingly.'

Once again, our anxiety was as palpable as our hopes were high until Huber, as per usual, cut through all our babbling and tried to raise his voice above the noise from the engines. Turning towards those whose demeanour might, according to him, have spelled distrust or fear, and I certainly was one of them, he tried reassuring us. 'Guys, don't shit in your pants. This bloke hasn't been decorated with the Iron Cross for nothing. He's made it quite clear that with us behind the Tigers we have nothing to fear.' Some of us couldn't help remembering the Russian infantry and therefore remained sceptical.

The driver first steered the tank along the right-hand side of the field then veered towards its middle. The other three tanks positioned themselves as per directives. While our Tiger was turning, I could see from the corner of my eye a swarm of T-34s breaking out of the forest and with a roaring noise ripping through the air they thundered towards us.

'So many?' I was dismayed. 'How will our four Tigers ever keep them away!'

'Seems they've been waiting for us,' stated our poacher with his shrill voice sounding even shriller through all the noise. 'Are we to be mashed into pulp under their tracks?'

'Silence!' yelled an irate Huber. It had obviously got to him as well.

Our Tiger fired its first shot and the others followed suit. While peering across to the enemy from behind our tank I could hear four distinct shells crashing into their targets. Four dark pillars of smoke rose above four Russian tanks that had instantly burst into flames, with our poacher, his voice hoarse with excitement, laconically stating that there now were four fewer tanks for us to contend with. 'But guys,' he complained, 'there are more and more appearing from out of the forest!' Tension grew further. 'These T-34s are firing with MGs as well,' gasped Richard.

'Of course! Stay close behind the Tiger!' bellowed Huber with our tank at that same moment lurching forward and firing. Another T-34 exploded some 200 metres in front of us. But the impact of anti-tank shells crashing into the front plates of our Tiger, though not piercing it, left us shaken to the core. Our Tigers obviously suffered no damage as they continued to fire relentlessly, systematically, accurately. We could hardly believe it. Every shot a hit. The enemy, however, appeared undaunted and they too bombarded us mercilessly with more shells hailing down on, but fortunately ricocheting off, the armour plates of our Tigers. The deafening cacophony of noise from the blasting shell fire, thundering engines and the crashing of explosions all built up to a thunderous inferno the likes of which I had never heard before.

'German workmanship!' Heinz Weber yelled into my ear, hardly able to get his words heard above the detonations.

'There are fifteen on fire, if I haven't miscounted.'

'You haven't – I got the same number. Bet you they won't dare come any closer. They're banging away like mad, but aren't getting anywhere!'

'Thank God, there's no infantry!'

'What's happening here today is something to behold!'

'We've never seen Tigers, let alone in action – we've only ever heard about them.'

Crouching behind the tank, rifles in hand and ready to fire, we jubilantly counted the hits while breathing in the exhaust fumes. We dreaded the moment we would hear the terrifying '*Urrah!*' from the infantry which had sent a chill to our bones so many times before. But it didn't happen.

Pressed tightly against the skirt of the Tiger which steadily rolled forward towards the forest while ferociously pounding the enemy with fire, we caught sight of burnt-out or still smouldering T-34s strewn to the right and left of us. From some of them hung charred corpses covered in tattered uniforms slumped over the edge of the hatches, head-down. I asked myself how old these men might have been. Fleetingly wondering about their mothers, their pain and their tears, I gulped. But then another hissing and booming noise. An explosion detonating only some fifty metres away from where I was, with flames shooting out of a crumbling T-34, made me break out in a cold sweat.

Covered in grimy soot from the Tiger's emissions, practically numb with exhaustion, we nevertheless felt a sense of satisfaction, one which until then we hadn't ever experienced. Never in our wildest dreams had we expected this astonishing victory.

At long last, I thought, finally the day had come when the Russians had seriously miscalculated their opponent, and I had been a part of it. I tried counting how many tanks we had finished off, but kept starting from scratch and then gave up.

From up above me I suddenly heard the voice of the Iron Cross bearer, we never did find out his name, shouting down from the turret: 'The Russians are clearing out – they're giving up. Our shots did it – they couldn't cope! Let's move – we'll chase them into the forest! But attention! We're short of fuel and can't afford to go far. Our ammunition – precious – is also running low. Stay close behind, boys. The ride might get bumpy. Watch out for enemy infantry – to your right and left!'

After putting behind us some twenty or thirty metres bulldozing across flattened tree trunks, one of the Tiger's tracks suddenly snapped. 'Puts an end to our advance, I'd say,' grumbled Huber into his soot-covered stubble. 'Would have been a pretty show, shame that.'

'Provide fire protection! We've got to tow the Tiger away!'

'Provide fire protection to whom?' asked Richard. 'Tell you what, Hans,' he said. 'We can bluff, pretend that we're inspecting the building to our right there. Come along with me!'

'But don't go any further than that!' we heard Huber shout. We had already turned to leave, not before marvelling open-mouthed at the speed with which the crew had attached the defective tank to the tail part of the other one with the help of some steel tow ropes.

Once we stood in front of the barn, Richard unbolted the door and, sliding it slowly to the side, we both held our guns ready to shoot. We would have expected anything but what we saw, only dimly at first as it was half-dark inside. The scene that came into our view was so horrific it made our blood run cold. Young women and girls of all ages crouched or stood on the cold, heavily trodden, mud floor, terror in their eyes. On recognising us as German soldiers they started screaming in what seemed to me one massive wail.

'Germans, praise the Lord!'

'Are they gone? Are the Russians gone?'

'Who', Richard tried to shout over the women's cries, 'put you in here?' I couldn't get a word past my lips.

An older, quite well-dressed woman in riding gear planted herself in front of Richard and, lifting her arm up to command silence, she offered to speak for the rest. 'The Russians caught up with our convoy. They carted off our men and children, and all our belongings on our sledges, and took them away. Eastwards again. Us, they herded together and should anyone try and escape, they threatened to shoot them on the spot … but now,' she barely stopped to breathe, 'we couldn't make out what was happening outside for all the deafening noise and not being able to see anything – and we kept thinking that there were Russian soldiers on guard outside'.

A woman stepped right up to me, grabbed my arm and screamed that the Russians had deported her father-in-law and children to the east. Her voice then failed her. More and more women were spilling out of the shed when I heard the captain of the tank squad asking how many women there were. '198,' reported the first woman, '198 women and girls, captain!'

'Take them back and have them gather in an orderly fashion behind that building over there. I'll organise trucks to have them transported to safety.'

It was only then that I noticed that all the women and girls were wearing trousers underneath their coats. Some of them, too weak to walk and keep pace with the younger ones, looked forlorn and helpless. I picked up an old grannie of some seventy years and supported her to the location the officer had assigned. What a wretched bunch of dazed women this was, I thought, dragging their stiff bodies out and slowly winding their way between the bullet-riddled T-34s towards the collection point.

The last ones of the convoy had finally made it when Richard, who had supported a younger pregnant woman, gave all those gathered some comforting news. 'Seems that a radioed message of an Iron Cross holder can be counted on. Over there, look, wouldn't you know it – four trucks!'

By then, it was early afternoon and it didn't take long for the 198 women and girls to find a seat or spot on the cargo platforms to hold themselves tight, when the trucks and their live cargo departed.

'Thank goodness for that – we just about managed to avert a mass rape,' mumbled Richard but the danger did not seem to be over yet. 'Listen up everyone!' shouted our sergeant. 'We've been ordered to stay put and wait for new instructions. All of you – pay utmost attention! Yes, the Russians have had a setback, but they can attack at any moment, as in the meantime their infantry have most certainly caught up with them. Whatever has been salvaged from our baggage will have been deposited on the eastern outskirts of Königsberg. My guess is that we should eventually make our way in that direction. Huber!'

'Present, sergeant!'

'Set up guard duty and as for the rest – organise them in teams to fan out and find something to eat!'

'Yes, sergeant!'

Sarge then stomped through the snow towards his lodgings which were in the farmhouse nearby. Again, I was put in the first rota, this time with Private Hans Reich. We had been tasked to guard the barn with the sliding door, but first I paid a visit to my four-legged friend in his partition. The gelding, still anxious and stomping on his robust legs, snorted contentedly on recognising me. Perhaps it was the warm welcome of the animal which made me suddenly doubt the victory we had just achieved. Perhaps peace was only wishful thinking.

Returning to Hans Reich, I found that he too felt insecure and depressed, rather than elated by our success. 'I'd feel a hell of a lot more reassured if the Tigers were still around.'

I could only agree. By now acutely aware of the shortages the army was experiencing in just about every area but above all in armaments, I lamented the fact that, generally, there were too few Tigers. 'Who knows where they're being deployed at this moment?' I asked Richard, who muttered as usual into his well lined camouflage jacket, while slapping together his thickly gloved hands. I too had a pair like that to my name, I thought gratefully, while an icy wind whipped our faces.

Two stools stood in front of the sliding door, so we both sat down for a while silently staring out into the winter night which had come in early. My companion was six years my senior and wore the so-called *Gefrierfleischorden* in his button-hole – proof that he had lived through the infamous 1941/42 winter freeze on the Eastern Front. His silver *Nahkampfsspange,* his *Sturmabzeichen,* plus the Iron Cross 1st and 2nd Classes which were fastened to his breast pocket, certainly made me respect and admire this swashbuckler.* At that moment, in fact, his presence had a calming impact on me. He was reassuring. Hans, I thought to myself, if you stay close to him, not much can happen to you. That guy will always get out alive.

I had found out that he hailed from Isen in Upper Bavaria, was the son of a small farmer and had been apprenticed in the plastering trade, before being called up by Prussia's Glory. Chatting about trivial stuff, smoking a few cigarettes behind cupped hands, our two hours' guard duty flew by.

The following morning Moser took roll call. Our pitiful lot was a far cry from the dead-straight line-up on the barracks' quadrangle, but our sergeant didn't seem to care much.

'Good morning!' he greeted us, and we responded in kind. 'Good morning, sergeant.'

'I've received orders: leave at 1100 and make our way to the eastern outskirts of Königsberg. Lieutenant Hartmann will be expecting us there along with the rest of our baggage.' More relaxed in our general

---

* The *Gefrierfleischorden* ('Order of the Frozen Flesh', or more formally the *Ostmedaille* = Eastern Medal) was awarded for participation in the winter fighting on the Eastern Front in 1941–42. *Nahkampfsspange* = Close Combat Badge; *Sturmabzeichen* = General Assault Badge.

behaviour, we immediately started chatting among ourselves when the sergeant, once more adopting his usual air of command, raised his voice. 'All guards, attention! First rota to take their breakfast now. I've been told that this is the last of our supply, but we have farm bread, scrambled eggs with ham and, yes, some real coffee, which our poacher located in the villa yesterday. Dismissed!'

We didn't tarry. Together with Huber, Moser and five others, we bounded into the kitchen filled with the aroma of the wonderful brew. 'Heavens above!' exclaimed someone, addressing the poacher. 'Too bloody bad that God only created one of you! Where did you manage to unearth so many eggs?'

'No big deal – and they were still warm from the nest! Me and Reich went to this way-out farmstead, over there at the edge of the forest. Of course, we were careful. I believe that part of the estate consisted of a chicken farm. The long and short of it is, we bundled up as many eggs as we could in the sacks we found lying around and prepared them for your meal. There you go, *guten Appetit!*'

'What about the real coffee?'

'No explanation, why's it my fault that you're either too stupid or too lazy to have a good look around? Pity that we have to leave today. Yesterday, on my wanderings, I came across a pretty well stocked wine cellar. Helped me go to sleep after guard-duty!'

'Listen, wise-guy. If I come across one of you lot tipsy or indeed drunk, I must report him. Everyone knows what he can expect!' That was Moser being officiously annoyed.

'Certainly, sergeant sir! Being court-martialled is probably the only thing which still works nowadays!' Reich was equally irate but his comment at least got mumbled approval from the rest of us.

I wasn't the only one who enjoyed a plentiful breakfast that morning. Before making space for the next shift, I tucked a large piece of the black bread into my jacket pocket and as for the wine, I decided I could really do without it.

But I was taken aback when Moser caught us unawares with his orders. 'Huber, take two men and plant however many mines we've got left along the path leading to the wine cellar. But let everyone know when you've completed the job. We're certainly not going to leave this for the Russians!' Whether or not Huber managed to squirrel away one or two bottles prior to carrying out his mission, I never found out.

When we departed promptly at 1100 we were a sorry sight to behold. All heroic bravado had disappeared. After marching for some two hours we came to a clearing in the wood and heard a tremendous crash. An unexpected Russian artillery attack forced us to throw ourselves flat on the ground and take cover – something we had grown quite accustomed to by now. I pressed myself down hard in the snow, buried my head between my shoulders and could hear the splintering howl of detonating shells spraying shrapnel into the air.

Damn, I thought to myself, these explosions sound horribly close. Do Russians have eagle eyes? Are they able to spot us?

'I'm hit!' I heard someone wail. 'My foot!'

Someone else near me was moaning in pain. 'Man, my upper thigh . . . mush. Don't leave me, I beg you!' he beseeched everyone and no one.

Just as suddenly as the attack had begun, it fell silent. There must only have been ten or fifteen separate explosions, but we had suffered four injured soldiers, whom we patched up as best we could at the edge of the field. Richard, crouching next to me, did his utmost – but it wasn't good enough. 'Not my fault, I only have one first-aid kit left, hardly any dressings . . . we can't afford many more such surprises.'

My own supply had also run low and I could only nod. Moser then gave the order for one man to remain with the wounded until somebody could come and pick them all up. 'We'll look after you,' he assured them, 'and I don't want to hear any moaning and groaning!'

The rest of us twenty-seven downtrodden men continued on. I was just glad that I was amongst them. Having to lie out there in the cold was not what I fancied doing.

My legs had been bothering me for a while. I had noticed that I no longer had any feeling in my feet, wrapped in soaked-through and half-frozen felt boots. But since I could still hold myself upright and walk, I silently hoped that by continuous movement I would eventually regain sensation.

That afternoon around 1500 we reached the first houses on the outskirts of Königsberg. With the bare branches of a group of ancient-seeming crooked oak trees tangled up together and reaching high into the sky, the landscape seemed bleak, barren and threatening. A few snowflakes fluttered to the ground. That's where our baggage had been deposited, lying in wait on one of the last trucks of what had once been an impressive fleet. All the others had been demolished by the Russian shells which had hailed down during the past few days. While I believed that mines were being stored in the truck and I wasn't sure where the baggage was, what actually concerned me more was seeing our Lieutenant Hartmann standing tall and erect and instructing our sergeant who disappeared around a corner. He then returned.

'Hartmann will send a pickup truck to rescue the injured and the guard.' Moser told us and then urged us to seek shelter for the night somewhere around the neighbourhood. 'People are said to be quite friendly,' he continued, 'so you shouldn't encounter too many problems. I've already managed to get myself a camp bed with Hartmann and the chief of the infantry.' Aha, I thought, so he's all sorted. 'But,' ordered Moser, 'don't move too far away from each other. We're to report here tomorrow morning at 0800. We're to recapture Neuhausen and its airfield. Some infantry and perhaps even an assault gun battalion will back us up.' That was not all. Moser now launched into the next part of the order he had been given. 'We're to clear the airfield with the help of tractors – already requested – and that should pave the way for cargo planes to land and supply us with the reinforcements we so desperately need. Good news, right?'

We mumbled approvingly. From the corners of our eyes we saw a pickup truck, its platform filled with straw, appear and rattle past us in the direction from which we had just come.

'Well, by Jove! They're true to their word – the injured will be rescued in no time,' said Richard with obvious pride and the poacher chimed in equally enthusiastically. 'If all this works out equally smoothly tomorrow – well, perhaps we still stand a chance of winning this war!'

'Oh, silly boys that you are!' someone exclaimed, 'Give us a hand, will you, to find some proper lodgings for us lot. Who the hell knows what tomorrow will bring?'

It didn't take Richard and me very long to find somewhere to stay the night. In the second house down a small lane a war widow and her father-in-law took us in with open arms. Each of us got a bed and they even turned the boiler on. Our two hosts in fact seemed to compete with each other as to who could do more to make us feel welcome in their home. The electricity had gone out and so that evening, washed and clean-shaven, Richard and I sat with our new family at a candle-lit table enjoying the traditional Königsberg dish of dumplings with caper sauce along with crispy fried gold-yellow potatoes. No, these people were not wealthy, but they wished to offer us the best from what they owned. In East Prussia, they explained, generosity towards guests has been an age-old custom.

What we couldn't share was their optimism and their confidence that these widely praised miracle weapons would work. We had first-hand experience of how powerful the Russians were and that they were practically standing at our doorstep. While Richard confided in them and informed them of our mission to join other units and launch a counter-attack, I couldn't quite hide my misgivings.

Meanwhile my feet didn't do too well with my toes having turned a blue-reddish colour and being uncomfortably itchy. Utterly exhausted, however, I nodded off and in fact slept so deeply that Richard had to wake me the following morning so we would be on time for the roll call.

After a hearty breakfast we shouldered our rifles and made our way back up the alleyway with our hosts' genuinely expressed Godspeed ringing in our ears. After just a few steps we froze. Shells came whizzing past, exploding in the square in front of us. The 'morning greeting' lasted but a minute and Richard didn't seem fazed in the least. 'Couldn't have been meant seriously,' is all he muttered. Then, quickening our pace and lifting our heads, we certainly got the shock of our lifetime. Our truck, loaded with mines, had been hit by one of the shells, but, contrary to what one might have expected given its explosive cargo, the vehicle itself didn't actually blow up. Instead, each one of the mines detonated based on its respective type and construction, illuminating the sky and engulfing the square. Amidst the cacophony of crashing, howling and bursting we stared at the freshly carved white wounds that had been torn into the tree trunks of the nearby oaks. The fire rapidly spread, igniting the boxes containing explosives, and a huge yellow-red fireball flared up, ripping the vehicle into a myriad splinters hurled into the air as debris of stone and wood hailed down.

'That's it then, Hans!' remarked Richard sarcastically. 'Looks like the Russians have no need for miracle weapons, they can well manage without.'

'I've driven this b— b— beauty for nearly three years now,' I heard its driver now standing next to me stutter. 'Now this?'

'Just thank your lucky stars!' the poacher who had joined us admonished him. 'Obviously, your time isn't up quite yet and so you'll just have to march along like the rest of us.'

'Silence!' ordered the sergeant. 'Attention! The word is that the generals are putting together a special plan to retake that airfield. Then we can clear it. We're expecting to hear further!'

Gathering in small clusters, many of us just stared at the ground. While some chatted in hushed tones, I was left with a strange sensation. I didn't recognise it. Never before, not throughout my entire time at the front, had I felt like this. Was it fear? Surely, I wasn't any more anxious than before any other deployment during the war? Something foreboding, something intangible and sinister grabbed hold of me. Turning to Hans Reich standing in my group, I asked him a big favour. 'Hans, Isen, where you're from – that isn't too far from Munich, is it? Can you be sure to tell my mother should something happen to me today.'

Putting his hand on my shoulder he just grinned. 'Sure, of course, I'll definitely do that, silly man.' And then, more facetiously: 'Caught a touch of front fatigue, have you? I'm familiar with it – have seen action for years . . . but it doesn't mean a thing. Get a grip of yourself, comrade, and don't shit in your pants. Nothing will happen to you today either.'

Everyone who had overheard our brief conversation averted their eyes. Nobody laughed. We drew our last puffs on our cigarettes, exchanged a few comments about nothing in particular and waited. This was not the calm before the storm. We all knew what that was like, but this here was different. This wait was more arduous and more nerve-racking than any other. Finally, a motorcycle messenger hurtled towards us, stopped in front of Moser and handed him some document or other, then turned his bike around and whizzed off.

Our sergeant, briefly scanned the piece of paper, then turned to us as we waited expectantly for what he might say. 'There's a delay . . . the assault-gun battery has been held up,' he said in a deliberately neutral tone of voice. 'But they'll catch up with us. We're to set out at once. The smallest delay . . . and we'll endanger the mission. From single file to single column, facing to the right!'

A box filled with three rockets for an *Ofenrohr* was shoved into my hand with Richard officiously declaring that he was trusting these to me. 'You'll have to craft your own tube, mind you, and some sort of sling to transport this little lot,' he added, 'and when the Russians approach, you just empty them all into their tanks.' Thank goodness the box had heavy string handles on its side, which I removed, tying one end around my thick gloves and the other to the box. Relieved to have some anti-tank ammunition, I dragged the box through the snow.[*]

There had never been an occasion nor a time when we had followed an order so listlessly and with less attention to detail as on that day, even though we were at long last pushing forward. Sure, it was a welcome change from the repeated and disheartening withdrawals of the past weeks, but was it too little too late, I wondered. Slowly, cautiously, we trudged through the trampled snow. There was nobody around. From where we were across the vast terrain and up to the edge of the forest nothing was moving.

With our teeth grimly clenched throughout, it must have been two hours that we stomped through the area which had seemingly

---

[*] *Ofenrohr* ('stove pipe') was a slang term for the *Panzerschreck* anti-tank weapon, similar to the Allied bazooka. It is unclear why Fackler would take the trouble to carry the ammunition if the firing tube was missing.

been deserted by both friend and foe. The poacher broke the silence. 'I'm not always right, but it's pretty obvious that there's been some fierce fighting going on around here while all of us were sound asleep . . . Not for a moment do I believe that there aren't any Russians close by.'

The lifeless body of a Landser lying in our path, his limbs twisted and his helmet askew covering half his face, proved the poacher's words true. Bullets had penetrated his chest and neck and dark red blotches stained the snow around his corpse. His wide-open eyes stared to the sky.

'Would you believe it . . . his comrades must have only been able to pick up the wounded . . . But where the hell are the Russians? Where have they disappeared to after leaving this mess?'

We got the order to track them down. 'Fan out, cordon off the area, push forward!'

We had barely moved at all when the air was filled by shells whizzing and hissing past our ears, spraying mud, snow and sparks in all directions. As so often before, I flung myself into a burrow which must have expertly been dug by some Landser now long gone. With Hans Reich close to me, I felt safe.

'Shit! Our fine leaders certainly kept mum – not a word spilled that Russians were lying in wait for us!' he scoffed. 'Reinforcement coming our way? Makes you laugh . . . they can't be trusted for a moment, not a moment. So now . . . we've got to take the hit.'

His eyes were now fixed on the box of *Ofenrohr* ammunition that I held clamped between my knees. He ordered me to discard it. 'Out!' he yelled, 'or do you want the both of us to be blown into smithereens? And besides – nobody has a clue where the tube has gone.' Without giving it another thought I flung the box outside.

Night had fallen. Leaning back against the wall of the pit, which had been moulded into a seat, I stared towards the edge of the forest. 'Hans, are those dark spots over there T-34s?'

'Absolutely. I doubt they'll roll any closer today, but I swear they'll join the shoot-out if what we're hearing is any indication.'

In the meantime, however, the thunderous explosions diminished and eventually died down altogether. I could see Reich's eyes gleam and suddenly he leapt up out of our cover and sprinted backwards. Perhaps he thought I would follow him, but for a split-second I hesitated, not being able to decide whether I should. Outside it wasn't exactly pitch dark what with the snow shimmering in the night and I feared being spotted by the T-34s, which were less than about 400 metres away. But then, I made a dash for it and was running as fast as my numb feet could carry me.

CHAPTER 6

The Last Shell

The fierce shelling around me became even more ferocious and had me hopping like a hunted hare in zig-zag lines across the frozen snow. Were they targeting me? Suddenly, a sharp burn on the inside of my left thigh travelling to my stomach and up to my face forced me to the ground doubled-up in pain. I must have fainted then.

I am not sure how long I lay sprawled out in the open field, probably one or two hours before I became aware of blinking stars high above the clear winter sky. I tried to pull myself up, but realised that neither my legs nor my arms were moving. I also had the strange sensation that part of my nose was limply hanging over my lips. It seems unbelievable but, despite the bitter cold, I felt warm inside and apart from a profound loneliness pressing on my heart, nothing seemed to hurt. Was it a hallucination, I wondered, when a German medic, shoulders hunched, scurried across the terrain. I cried for help and couldn't believe my eyes when the man actually stopped short, changed direction and approached me. Kneeling he put down his bag.

'Stay nice and still, comrade. Are there more behind you?'

'I doubt it, I think I was the last one who got out.'

'First, let me put your nose back where it belongs, I've got bandages. You can count yourself lucky, man, the blood has fortunately congealed with this cold and you've now got a firm crust.'

He then busied himself and put a dressing on my shrapnel wounds, on my thigh, my stomach, my right arm and right hand. 'Yup, it sure got you good,' he whispered in a soothing voice, 'but I'd say it's a sight better than dying a hero's death. Be careful . . . your jacket and gloves are full of splinters. Now, can you walk? I know your feet must be completely frozen – let's try and make it to my cart.'

When he gripped my arm to sling it around his neck and pull me upright, a searing pain shot right through my body as if I had been pricked by a hundred needles. And yet, even though the whole of my legs were frozen right down to the toes, they took my weight. It is surprising what one can achieve by sheer determination. Hobbling back the 600-metre distance to a barn I gratefully spotted a horse and cart with a single horse in the shafts, presumably belonging to the grand estate. Once again I came across the Landser who had been shot dead during our advance. Or was it another one? The medic's words referring to the misconception of a hero's death struck me deeply. How right he was. No, I thought to myself, it's not my turn yet and with that I heaved my poor body up onto the cart, slumping down next to some other seriously wounded guys who lay there groaning and whimpering. Quietly, but rather satisfied, I settled into the soft cushioning of the lordly vehicle.

The medic jumped onto the coach seat. Turning around to tell us that on the way we would pick up another wounded soldier, he assured us that it was possible despite how cramped we already were. 'He can squeeze in here next to me.'

In the meantime, not a single shot had been fired. Where were the enemy hiding? Were the Russians taking a nap behind their armour plates? Our good medic, lightly clicking his tongue, gently flicked his reins over the horse's back and with that the sledge glided softly along the straight alleyway, past the gnarled trunks of the oak trees.

I probably wasn't the only one in that cart who felt he had escaped death by a hair's breadth and been granted this blissful ride through a winter's night – but it wasn't to last. Soon we heard what by now had become the familiar sound of shells whistling through the air. It didn't take me long to calculate that some of them would likely explode in our vicinity. From behind I could see the medic's back tense up, struggling to tame the frightened animal which was rearing up. Then the horse took off, wildly galloping into the wood, in and among the trees, dragging the sledge behind so that it skidded sideways throwing us into a heap, often just missing one of the heavy tree branches by a fraction.

What? Would it be my fate to suffer death under the runners of a sleigh instead of from a bullet?

Desperately I tried to grab the side of the sleigh with my unhurt hand to avoid being hurled to the ground. Several times more the sleigh skidded precariously, balanced on one runner and nearly toppled over. My heart was in my mouth. Having put behind us a small hilltop, we veered downwards at reckless speed. But what was that? A Landser, dressed in a long winter coat, his arm holding a stick stretched out straight in front of him, was planted smack in the middle of the narrow pathway. He stood there motionless. Three, four seconds later the horse – nothing short of a miracle to my mind – bucked, very nearly unhinging the cart, but then came to a halt just in front of the soldier, snorting and trembling all over. Calmly, all the while whispering softly, the soldier stroked its mane, and the horse seemed to listen intently, pricking up first one ear, then the other and, visibly reassured, it settled. I saw steam rising from its flanks.

'Don't worry,' I heard the Landser addressing the animal while lightly tapping its neck, 'I know you aren't used to all this banging about.'

None of this lasted more than half a minute. Climbing up with a short groan, the Landser then perched himself on the coach seat. I noticed that one of his sleeves was loosely tucked into his coat pocket, and judging from his bulky upper body, I gathered he was wearing his arm in a sling. Truth be told, I didn't much care either way. We'd had a lucky escape and that's all that counted. The guy next to me was unconscious and so had missed this ride from hell but the other three men wouldn't stop blabbering. For just a moment their injuries seemed forgotten.

'I sure as hell could see myself sliced into bits underneath the runners of the sleigh!'

'Me too!'

'This kind of hero's death ain't for me . . . last thing I needed after what I've been through.'

I took a deep breath and could only comment that, once again, I had scraped through.

Our real hero, meanwhile, the guy who had tamed the horse, turned to the medic and quietly asked to take over the reins. 'I can handle that with one hand, have no fear, after all, I've been raised on horses.'

On it went, this time with our horse at walking pace, but gradually, neighing once loudly into the night, it changed to a gentle trot.

Eventually we reached a barn and spent the rest of the night huddled into a corner, atop a meagre supply of straw. Huffing and puffing, the medic managed to yank off my boots which were frozen stiff and then swaddled my legs and thighs with thick pieces of cloth which he had magically pulled out of his bag. Dawn had broken when a truck stopped in front of the barn. Two burly men descended, heaved me and the others onto the open cargo bed and once again we burrowed into some flattened straw. I have no idea how long we rumbled through the area. It was a chilly morning and still early when we arrived in a place called Fischhausen,* according to my neighbour. 'It's a collection point,' explained one of my other companions, 'they've turned the church into a temporary first-aid station intended to take care of scattered soldiery.'

A sergeant, again one of those intimidating 'chain dogs', stood right in the centre aisle, and, true to form, was bossing the staff around and giving out orders as if he were in a train station. 'Straw beds located in front of what once was the altar, right in the front of this space,' he bellowed, 'they're for you – now off with you!'

My having been knocked around continuously for hours on that truck, the crusts covering my wounds had split open and I was feeling nauseous.

'Why don't you sit yourself down, right here, on the step to the altar,' suggested a kindly older medic whose green uniform was protected by a long surgeon's gown tightened by straps tied behind his back and only leaving some space at the bottom for his army boots to peep out. Whist his voice was soothing and comforting, his blood-splattered gown was less so. Trying as best I could to muffle my groaning, I sank onto the allocated spot.

---

* Now Primorsk, Russia.

With a few expert hand movements the medic removed my sleeve, briefly made eye-contact with me and, while busying himself with some instruments, explained to me what was going to happen next. 'Nope, we have nothing to anaesthetise you, so we'll have to perform an emergency operation on your arm without it. But', he quickly added, all the while disinfecting a small area in the crook of my arm with the strong whiff of alcohol stinging my injured nose, 'it won't be too awful looking at it.' The jab with the syringe swiftly followed with the medic informing me that this was morphine. 'Bizarrely, we have plenty of that,' he mumbled and that in his opinion this was by far preferable to an anaesthetic. 'Much better for you, works for way longer. Sure, you might be a bit dozy afterwards, but at least you won't be feeling any discomfort.'

Once finished with his procedure, I could still hear, faintly, his comment that it might take a while until it was my turn. 'There are just so many of you guys pouring in, and that's with our chain dog out front there making quite sure that only very few are admitted to this section. Just have a lie-down in the meantime.'

And while still speaking to me, he turned his back to lean down to the Landser waiting behind me who was crying out in pain.

Obediently, totally exhausted, I stretched out on the straw spread out in front of the altar. No, it certainly cannot be said that my hospital bed was clean – nothing even close to it. It was a filthy pile of waste over which hung a putrid smell of blood, pus and other disgusting excretions – but I didn't let that bother me. At long last, I could rest and I felt deep gratitude for the medical care I was about to receive. A brief glance at the vestry to my right, however, with the door slightly ajar, put me on guard as that was where soldiers were being operated on. Loud wailing, desperate sobbing which then all of a sudden tapered down to a small whimpering and eventually died down altogether told me that the medical care I was so longing for might not turn out to be so appealing. I imagined that it could well be someone lying unconscious under the knife undergoing an amputation. The door fell shut.

It certainly made me slightly anxious, but at the same time it didn't actually scare me outright and so I decided not to worry further.

Could the morphine have already kicked in? That surely must have been it, I told myself, as when my eyes travelled upwards towards the angels above the altar, I believed they were actually floating towards me with their wings spread out and smiling kindly.

The harsh voice of the Feldgendarmerie sergeant rudely tore me out of my reveries. 'Of course you're fit for service,' he hollered, 'What the hell are you pretending! Out! Back to the front, you miserable draft dodger!'

'Why are you yelling?' someone asked, his tone stern and commanding, but controlled. 'Stop that right now! These men don't deserve this. There surely must be another way to encourage them to continue fighting! And by the way, what we've got here in front of us are seriously injured soldiers – they should not have to tolerate this racket you're making!'

From the sounds of it, this man must have out-ranked the chain dog substantially as for a while things in the back of the church did calm down. Then it was my turn, and supported by a medic I limped into the vestry, that is into the surgery section.

'What's wrong with your legs? Frostbitten? Let me have a look before we cut.'

I barely felt the rags being removed from my legs. I assumed that my frostbites were first being treated with an ointment. Actually I could only guess what was being done to me and concluded that my legs were being bandaged.

'The nose has been put back into place beautifully,' declared the young doctor, obviously impressed. 'Did a doctor do that?'

'Nope, it was a medic!'

'Well, my friend, in this case, you sure lucked out with him. You'll have a scar, but your sniffer seems to be in good shape and it'll straighten out. But we'll have to remove some of the large bits of shrapnel which you've caught.'

Despite my morphine-induced daze I often screamed in pain, when the doctor apparently didn't just remove the shrapnel but also dug into several infected wounds which I had suffered on my upper thigh and abdomen. 'Hold tight for another couple of minutes,' urged the doctor, gouging deeper, 'we'll be finished soon.' My brain still befuddled, I could barely register his voice trailing off. 'Give him another dose. He can tolerate it,' is what I heard last.

The rest of the day saw me and another four comrades lying on the straw-covered floor of a small barn, probably part of the parish garden. It's difficult to recall the next night exactly, but I woke up the following morning to see a medic standing in front of us.

'Boys, you're the fortunate ones. You're being picked up in a couple of minutes and will be taken to the port of Pillau* and from there you'll be travelling by boat going west. But let me first offer you some of our "special breakfast", that'll help you with your journey!' he said mischievously.

The five of us were elated – and not just because of the morphine breakfast – and were chattering incoherently.

'Military hospital?'

'Transport by ship?'

'Likely, this spells the end of the war for us lot.'

'Let the others enjoy the *Endsieg*, I could fancy going home without being forced to play the hero.'

Though happy, we still tried to keep our voices down, and probably sounded drunk. The extra dose we had just enjoyed seemed to have transported us into la-la land.

But the medic had also left behind – placed on top of the folded coat of my neighbour which he was using as a blanket – a portion of army bread and some artificial honey. With his pocket knife the comrade proceeded to slice off fairly equal slices which we passed down the line. Chewing on it, I noticed not actually being hungry, and just automatically moved my jaws up and down as if they didn't even belong to me. I was floating on clouds.

I couldn't say what time it was when, supported by a Landser, I hobbled to the truck and joined the other four – settling on the straw-covered cargo platform. I'm also still uncertain as to how long we travelled through the cold winter morning, with nothing protecting us in the frigid temperatures other than a few thin blankets. But one thing I do remember and that is that despite the relentless shoving

---

* Now Baltiysk, Russia.

and pushing during that journey, the pain I felt was far less acute than I had endured during my previous transports. I was grateful for the morphine.

Though driven at a snail's pace and though the road was precariously narrow, our vehicle overtook a stream of horse-drawn wagons, two-wheel hand-carts and sledges pulled by old women and young children. Horses' hooves slipped on the ice, wagons crashed and poorly constructed sleighs splintered. Mostly frail, these refugees, looking longingly at our vehicle, had obviously been driven from their homes and were now surging towards the port towns. Their carts, heaped with all kinds of household goods, clothing and carpets and even livestock, jammed the narrow road. The scene left a deep impression on me despite my brain fog. Why, I wondered, hadn't they fled beforehand? Hadn't they known that the Russians had been lurking on their doorstep for some time? So why the delay? Why this wretched flow of evacuees? What now? Now, they would all have to be put on a ship in order to avoid falling into the hands of the Russians.

CHAPTER 7

To Safety on the *Gustloff*?

Our truck parked so close to the pier I could hear waves softly lapping at the rocky wall while an order was issued: 'Take these five men to the first compartment of the barracks, right next to the door!' This was the senior lieutenant in charge, who then asked whether there were more injured to follow.

I couldn't catch what our elderly driver responded as by then I was concentrating on pulling myself into the barracks with the help of two medics, neither of them particularly strong men themselves.

'Boys,' rasped one of them, 'you don't know how incredibly lucky you are. If a ship arrives you guys are right now so far ahead in the queue that you'll stand a fair chance of being allowed on board. Our senior sergeant is a great guy – and he has purposely kept these barracks reserved for wounded army people.'

'Hannes,' scolded the other medic, 'why are you babbling non-sense and raising false hopes? Don't you remember the crushing crowds when a ship comes into port? The throngs of people shoving when trying to board? And why talk about boarding anyway . . . we have fewer and fewer boats coming in . . .'

'Sure, I know . . . but it could work.'

The barracks had been divided up into several compartments, with triple bunk-beds to either side of the door along the wall. What with the iron stove, a cylindrical structure in the middle of the room, working OK and me having been assigned the lowest bed, I felt close to being comfortable. Above me there was the Landser who had had his foot amputated and he was obviously in agony as he kept throwing himself back and forth on the planks groaning, apparently still delirious.

Early afternoon, it was 29 January, I finally woke up from my semi-consciousness and watched as the medic passed a piece of army bread and artificial honey to the guy above me, along with a large jug of something I couldn't make out and some cups. He then left us to it.

'I'm sorry,' my neighbour above groaned pitifully, 'I cannot slice anything for you guys this time around.'

'No worries,' responded Fritz softly – he was lying across from me. 'Just toss down your pocket-knife – I'll be able to manage cutting through these wedges, surely.'

This time I actually chewed the hard bread with relish, washing it down with big gulps of the lukewarm brew. The effect of the morphine seemed to have worn off and an hour later, when the medic enquired if he could do something for me and I admitted wanting something to dull my pain, he told us that he would drop by later. 'I must first attend to some injured women and children, and two older men, but don't fret . . . I'm just hoping that my bandages won't have run out by then.' With that he was gone.

He never returned, but I was still able to doze off. All of a sudden, though, I was wide awake because the guy above me was kicking so hard that the entire bed frame had started shaking.

'Hannes,' I yelled up to him. 'Have you gone mad? Who can sleep with such an earthquake going on?'

The kicking stopped almost instantly and once again I fell into a light slumber frequently interrupted by burning and throbbing aches in my upper thigh, my stomach and my right arm. When the medic finally found his way back to us early the next morning, Hannes was dead, and the man above him as well.

The medic flung his bag down on the mattress above me, ran out and brought back the senior lieutenant whom we had met only briefly the day before. Briskly they carted the dead bodies away. 'But,' I heard another neighbour mumble disbelievingly, 'Norbert was with me in the same company . . . all that time . . . gosh, his death was as quiet and soft as he was in life.'

We could hear scraping noises next door, where they were removing another corpse. The medic then returned, crouched down next to me and shot a load of morphine into the veins of my left arm.

Well,' he chuckled, 'looks like you do very well on this devilish stuff. Count yourself lucky that we actually have plenty of that in stock. This will last you several days, I'm sure, maybe even longer. Pleasant dreams, matey!'

On the afternoon of 30 January we could hear the din of voices shouting and a great commotion from the dock. I sat up to be able to hear better. 'Hans, a ship must have docked!' exclaimed my neighbour, full of excitement. I could only nod weakly. The healthy dose of morphine was still having an effect and I could barely make out anything through the fog that enveloped me. Meanwhile there were women screeching, men bellowing and children crying – a cacophony of hysterical shouting. Once in a while we could catch a word or two.

'Finally!'

'Stay close together!'

'Don't run away! Stay with mummy or grandma!'

At one point I thought I recognised the voice of our senior lieutenant who seemed hugely agitated. 'I need help! Now, straight away!'

Someone using a megaphone roared above the clamour. 'This is the captain of the *Wilhelm Gustloff* speaking. We are overcrowded and we cannot let anyone else on board. But there are more ships due to arrive. We'll have to wait here until tonight as during daylight we run the risk of attracting attention, and since our escort convoy has not materialised, we would be an easy target for enemy vessels operating in the region. I wish everyone safe passage!'

The scene remained stuck in my mind. Gradually all the shouting and screaming emerging from the barracks subsided, only to give way to a general sense of disappointment. Suddenly, the medic burst into our barracks, dragged me out of the bunk, slung my left arm around his neck and hauled me outdoors like a sack of potatoes. 'Looks like the crewmen up there want to give us a hand,' he explained panting, 'What we'll do is heave you up and across the side of the ship. You're next in line.' And that's what he did. 'You can thank our senior sergeant,' he puffed and stretched me out next to Fritz, mumbling something about us being the first stowaways.

At that moment a metal platform some fifty centimetres square came crashing down to the floor, landing right in front of my heavily bandaged feet. I wouldn't be able to say how many rough hands then grabbed me under my shoulders, shoved me into the iron cage and tightened a belt around my waist before slamming the small door shut. There I was, suddenly floating slowly upwards. Though still groggy on the morphine, I do remember marvelling at how vast this monster ship was and how I was being transported to the stern third of it.

With a slight jolt my basket paused. Then, dangling from a small crane, it swayed up and across the railing and past a lifeboat which seemed gigantic to my eyes. When the basket landed with a thump on the deck, strong sailors' hands gripped my upper body, and pulling me three, four metres down the gangway, shoved me into a windowless cabin, where, rather unexpectedly gently, they put me down on one of the mattresses spread out on the corrugated deck surface. A few minutes later I was joined by Fritz and another few men and I could clearly hear one of the crew-members commenting on our luck. 'I bet you that our captain would not believe his ears if he was informed that we've packed another three passengers into this ship.'

I would never find out why more injured army men were not allowed on board even though we had two empty spaces next to us, which would never be filled. Fritz assumed that perhaps the basket which had whisked us up had stopped working. 'Possible,' I mused, 'but unlikely,' I added without hiding my suspicion. 'I don't think that what just took place went unnoticed? I bet that our little journey caused a fight to break out . . . people might have literally killed each other to secure a spot in the basket. Perhaps, that was the reason it stopped functioning.'

'Good God, Hans, if you're right, the three of us have sure had one hell of an escape.'

'Yup . . . it all went so quickly.'

Strangely, we spontaneously decided not to dwell on this further. Someone had tucked a small pillow under my head and thrown a blanket over my feet. The crew obviously tried to make their passengers comfortable. For some reason the corrugated floor underneath the mattress was not at all cold and, once again, I was filled with relief and gratitude. This *Gustloff* most surely had saved me from the inferno on the front line. In the last few days our front must have miserably collapsed, I assumed, and this being the case I had also escaped the fate of becoming a prisoner of war. I had dreaded that above all else. Hans, I concluded, you're as safe here as in your mother's lap. Maybe, that's it, maybe this is the end of the war. With my fears laid to rest and still slightly under the influence of the morphine I finally fell asleep.

Suddenly the door was flung open making me sit bolt upright and tense all my muscles. It had turned dark outside. An infantry soldier with a head bandage and an eyepatch stood at the threshold and pleadingly enquired whether we had any room for him. 'An icy wind is blowing outside . . . can I come into your den?'

Not actually waiting for our response, he entered and settled down in a corner on a tarpaulin rolled into a bundle which I had noticed when there was still some daylight. He left the door open. 'Let's at least hear what's happening outside. I can tell you,' he reported, 'it's all getting a bit uncomfortable out there, people are agitated, the wounded are still being put in various berths, but I suspect we'll pull away any minute . . . I picked up that there'll be no protection convoy. We seem to have two captains, both with the same level of authority, but apparently, they disagree on stuff like whether to light up the boat or not. One guy thinks it's Christmas,' he expanded, chuckling, '. . . wants to deck out the place with light festoons to signal peace. It should alert the enemy that he's carrying refugees, civilians and injured, he claims. The other guy wants to sail under the cover of darkness, in total black-out conditions, and doesn't want to attract any attention.'

The Landser had barely finished his update, which he had rattled off without taking a breath, when we felt the floor underneath us trembling. 'What did you just say?' I heard a voice from the corner.

'The engines are churning . . . why would we need the escort anyway . . . This liner is not one to be messed with – you won't believe the speed it can pick up!'

The newcomer got up to leave but then briefly turned around to say that he would see what was what outside and return. Some three or four minutes later he came back. 'We've left the pier and are moving slowly,' he reported. 'But the people we've left behind . . . total chaos . . . they're desperate . . . throngs of refugees pushing and shoving, trampling on each other, it's crazy. I couldn't stand it any more . . . Will they be able to get themselves on another ship?' His question hung in the air until both Fritz and I nearly simultaneously blurted out: 'Let's hope so.'

I saw Fritz grinning from across the semi-dark cabin while pointing at his neighbour. 'Hans, this guy will be sleeping through his rescue.'

'Or he doesn't have the same tolerance for the morphine, as we both do, though it all seems to be quite unreal to me . . .'

'D'you know what the time is?'

'No, but my guess is that it's somewhere around 1800. The sun starts setting a bit later around this time in January, but it still gets dark relatively early.'

Was I just imagining things, or was Fritz actually having to force himself to speak clearly? He too didn't seem to be suffering any pain. Morphine! What a wonderful drug for the likes of us.

'So, is it true that there's no escort for our ship?' I asked the Landser sitting in his corner and his response couldn't have been any more convincing.

'Definitely, absolutely, just heard that our two captains are experienced seamen. The one who insisted on going out all festooned has obviously prevailed. All lamps on deck are burning bright. These men are experts and surely know the best course, so they'll be certain to stay clear of any mines. Everything else is not important, really! What on earth could happen to us? We're going to reach the west much faster and much more safely than anyone else.'

The Landser kept on talking, more to himself than to us. 'It's a fact though . . . Truth is that we aren't only carrying civilians and injured . . . Down there below, I could see with my own eyes the drained swimming pool, it was jam-packed with a bunch of young women auxiliaries. What's more, I also overheard two naval officers talking to each other and mentioning that a number of sailors attached to the 2nd Submarine Training Division are on board. And so, my friends,' concluded the Landser with some bitterness, 'this makes our peaceful light decoration something of a deceit. But, comrades . . . should we care?'

Fritz and I once again slipped into our morphine-induced dreams and dozed off contentedly with the steady rumbling of the ship's powerful engines calming our nerves. Just before nodding off completely I could hear our Landser ruminating about the course of the ship. 'Looks like our destination is Swinemünde,* but it seems to be impossible to get any exact information from the naval guys on this vessel.'

At some point a terrifying bang roused me from my sleep. An enormous detonation thundered through the vessel and reverberated long into the night – more powerful than any other detonation I had ever heard before. Simultaneously I could feel the floor underneath me jolting and could see our Landser rushing to the door while calling out. 'What the hell was that? There must have been something in front of us?'

'We've been hit by a torpedo – portside!' I heard some man yelling at the top of his voice.

'Sounds like this is going to be fun.'

'Are you mad? Is it a submarine?'

A few moments later there was another blast and we knew it could only have come from a torpedo hit and this time I knew I wasn't just imagining the shaking of the floor beneath me. 'Hans,' I thought to myself, frightened despite the drugs pulsing in my veins, 'is it your fate to drown like a rat?'

I was still shaken when a third torpedo hit the ship – this time it struck closer to where we were situated. Even though I was still befuddled by the drugs and experienced everything as if in a dream, I kept my ears covered against the deafening blasts from the explosion, which seemed to last for ages. Then, I felt a pair of strong hands grabbing me, tearing me out of my berth, hauling me through a passageway and heaving me across the rail where another pair

---

* Now Świnoujście, Poland.

of hands received me and then lowered me into a lifeboat, where I landed on top of others.

I felt I was in a nightmare. The boat was filling up – slowly or fast, it was impossible to tell – with wailing women, children, men and other injured passengers. Every so often I could hear someone bark above me: 'Stay back! Women, children and the injured come first! This boat is overloaded.'

Once, an officer fired his pistol into the air to instil some calm and order. But the frenzied stampede continued.

Somewhere I had read or heard that such lifeboats were equipped for sixty passengers. But there was no doubt in my mind that the boat was being packed way beyond capacity with more and more people, women, children, old men cramming in. When the davits gradually lowered us closer to the water and at the same time put more distance between us in the lifeboat and the side of the ship, I felt elated, but at the same time and the closer we got to the dark sea beneath us, I was petrified. Could it be my imagination or was the *Gustloff* actually starting to list to one side? Yup, I looked again, it was definitely listing to port.

The lifeboat cranked lower to the water – a menacing and alien black sheet.

A little way away another lifeboat swung from the davits and then smacked down on the water just seconds before us. The pale wintry night was lit up by flares and light from the portholes. Behind them we could make out the dark contours of heads crammed next to each other – a grotesque mass of human agony.

What happened next is hard to put into words, but the terror which filled me that night will forever be etched in my mind. Fear made me forget which of my limbs was injured and the freezing temperatures nearly paralysed me. With a heavy jolt that first boat capsized – the stern tipping and the passengers inside being dumped into the glacial water in one big clump. What had caused it? Had a rope snapped or did one of the davits collapse because of the overloading? I was never to find out.

Behind my back I could hear shouts of panic which gradually faded. At long last, we landed on water.

'Let's get away . . . fast . . . now! Everyone, move! Move away from the ship!' shouted a sailor who, I was informed later on, was standing at the stern of our dinghy – I am not sure today if it was a proper lifeboat – operating the rudder. 'Go! Go! It's life or death! We've got to steer this thing away . . . Can't you see that the ship has listed more and more?' By then the liner was nearly lying on its side. The severe list of the ship had shifted its centre of gravity. 'We have to get away! Nobody can tell what'll happen. Will she be able to resist rolling? Go! Every able body! Row! If the *Gustloff* sinks and we aren't out of her way, she will drag us down with her.'

'Oh, those poor people over there! In the other boat! They're desperate! Can't we help them?' a woman begged.

'No – we're packed! and if they start clinging to the gunwale – we're all going to capsize. The water is ice-cold. They'll drown, if they don't first freeze to death. Tragic – but true. I said row – row, or do you want to die as well? Row, as if there's no tomorrow!'

I couldn't tell who was sitting behind me, as I was rammed so tightly in between other occupants that I could only look ahead or to the side. Our lifeboat was turning, I could feel our overcrowded vessel veering away from the sinking liner. The sea by then was calm – and thank goodness for that, as our boat was lying so low due to the weight that water splashed over the gunwales and came sloshing inside, soaking the platform and us, and if had there been significant waves they would have pulled us beneath them. Still woozy on the morphine, I blocked out further thoughts.

When the cries for help died down, I realised that I was praying. I sent my fervent supplications to heaven, begging God to grant all the dying and drowning a quick end. Was that me all of a sudden becoming religious? Was it the drug?

Our lifeboat was at a safe distance from the sinking *Gustloff* and positioned abeam of it. About 500 metres of watery darkness separated us from the sinking liner. Because I had no watch and still was very much confused, I couldn't quite tell how much time had elapsed since the first torpedo had hit the hull of the ship. Had it been an hour? Longer than that? I also couldn't make out if any more lifeboats were being lowered from where the ship was lying on its side, but somehow, I was able to catch a glimpse of the deck of the *Gustloff* as it gradually and steadily rolled over and settled into the water, still filled with people howling. Every few seconds, or so it seemed, some of those desperate to escape, and obviously not able to claw their way to a lifeboat, tossed themselves into the heaving sea – individuals on their own, or a whole bunch of them in one go. I didn't see whether or not they were wearing any life vests.

Then, something appeared on the horizon. What was it? I couldn't believe my eyes when in the hazy glow of the night we could gradually identify the contours of a warship, her bow searing through the foaming waves.

'A German destroyer! She'll definitely be able to take loads of people on board!' It must have been a very old man who had said this. Someone familiar with the navy.

The cries, expectant at first, trailed off when it became clear that the ship was no longer approaching but sailed away and disappeared behind the stern of the *Gustloff*, which by then was dipping precariously close to the water.

The same man whose throaty voice had announced our would-be saviour ship could be heard again, though I still couldn't tell quite where he was located. 'Looks like our destroyer has been attacked! Another torpedo. Had she stopped or attempted rescue, I can tell you right now that she would've become a target for the Russian submarines ... we'd suffer even more dead. She absolutely had to clear out! Pity!' How it came about that this guy knew what had happened would remain a mystery to me.

At the beginning the *Gustloff* sank only gradually, its bow tipping and the stern rising, but then it all went very fast. I thought I was dreaming ... but others saw it as well: portholes at the stern of the ship, their lamps gleaming eerily in the night, danced around while the lights of the ship, probably switched on in the emergency, flared in one last glow casting spectral shadows. The piercing blasts of the siren must have drowned out the pitiful screaming and yelling of those desperate passengers still scrambling and fighting, panicking and shrieking for lost relatives who hadn't made it into a raft or who were freezing to death in the water, having either jumped, tumbled over the edge of the rescue vessel or been tossed into the glistening black water. The wailing of the siren stopped and the screams for help subsided. Women, men and children had fallen silent, literally dead silent.

Terrified, near immobilised, I stared at the dark arena of horror and watched the waves lapping over the tail of the liner. Was I mistaken, or could I spot a masthead rearing from the waters? Down below mothers and fathers had drowned, babies had instantly frozen to death and not a single one of us had been able to help. The memory of this scene would never leave me.

The booming voice of our helmsman cut through the silence. 'They will definitely have radioed the authorities with details as to our position. We'll stay put. Rowing would just be a waste of our energy. As far as I am aware, we're positioned in one of the most frequented water routes. Another ship will definitely pick us up eventually! Let's all remain calm and literally sit tight and hold on!'

It's possible that from among all the shipwrecked passengers afloat, and seeing as I was still delirious from the morphine, I was probably the one most willing to follow his request. Behind my back there was havoc but it immediately switched to anxious whispering after our guide's advice. Even today I marvel at how quiet we all were given the situation. Who could blame us? With our vessel alarmingly low down in the water, not even the hardiest of us could have been filled with confidence – but it prevented everyone from moving unnecessarily. We were drenched, our clothes frozen stiff.

Once, I heard a small pleading voice call over: 'Mummy, I need to pee!'

'Don't worry, Hanschen, your little trousers are full anyway, there's no toilet here, my love.'

'Let's just hope that the wind keeps at bay,' mumbled some woman behind me anxiously. Every now and then we saw one of the other boats flit by like a dark shadow, along the inky water surface. A light breeze blew over the calm sea.

I spent the rest of the night as if in a fantasy world. When dawn broke, our eyes beheld a carpet of dead people still clad in life-vests, with debris and wooden objects bobbing up and down beside them.

'How many were on board the ship?' a young woman must have mumbled this question out loud.

'Seemed more than 10,000 – or even more. That's just a wild guess.' Our helmsman had only whispered his response, but even I who was placed furthest away from him could hear him clearly. 'Just keep still,' he repeated, 'We stand a good chance of being picked up!'

Yet again soft mumbling broke out with one child asking: 'uncle, will it be long till we can go on another ship ?' 'Not long, boy,' the uncle replied, 'but just stay sitting nice and still next to mummy, there's a good lad.'

At some point I counted five other lifeboats, each so low in the water given the number of passengers and their sodden clothes that it threatened to tip.

I retreated into myself. I wouldn't call it sleep, it was rather an exhausted state of disquieted rest which, however, seemed to shorten the wait – more than perhaps the rest of the crew were able to do. I managed to turn my neck just once, enough to catch a glimpse of a group of glum-looking survivors staring into space. Some mothers stoically reassured their children, consoled whimpering babies; others, lost in thought, held them close to their chests rocking them to sleep.

CHAPTER 8

Rescue and Onward Journey

It must have been early afternoon when I was woken up by loud screams, women yelling and men hoarsely shouting over each other. The commotion had our boat dangerously rocking back and forth and our helmsman hollered at the lot of us. 'Silence! Don't move from your seats! Want to risk your lives? Want to drown at this stage? They'll pick us up without your yelling. Stay calm.'

'Are we safe?'

'Not yet, but soon.'

'Mummy, is grandpa somewhere here?'

'No, Heiner, boy, he had to stay on the *Gustloff*.'

Some hundred metres away from us, a small ship stopped alongside a lifeboat and I watched people clambering up a rope ladder or being hoisted aboard by the sailors. Reassured to an extent, I was more heartened when I spotted a much larger vessel behind that rescue ship heading towards us, barely causing a ripple in the quiet sea. Then it glided to a stop about ten metres away.

'Keep calm!' our helmsman appealed, 'Unless you really want to topple off? If all of you rush portside, we'll capsize! I want discipline. Stay put.'

All I cared about was to be allowed back onto a normal ship. While it was approaching, I could decipher the faded painted letters spelling out East Prussia – Naval Service.

'It's a cargo ship!' came the announcement of our shipmaster.

'Yup, and the other one, in front of us, is a minesweeper, gathering the others. There, I can even see a torpedo boat on the starboard side!'

'Grandpa, how come you know all of this?' A young, thin boy of about eight years old, holding his little sister by the hand and standing behind his mother, had asked the question. The mother meanwhile was cradling an infant in her arms. All three of the kids were bundled up in thick coats and woollen hats.

'Child, during the last war I served in the navy, so yes, I do know a thing or two.' I could hear him replying but was distracted by what was happening with the cargo ship. A small rectangular part of its portside opened and out slid a platform that was carefully lowered to near water level. Three or four crewmen descended from the hull and plucked up the first of our agitated group, wildly babbling women, children, several wounded Landsers on crutches and elderly couples. I was the last to be lifted up. A lanky sailor had jumped into our boat and supported me under my arms and there I was, close to the front of the platform, though still lurching back and forth.

We found ourselves tightly huddled together in the vast cargo hold; some, mostly women and children, sat there on benches, with their belongings stacked in front of them – rucksacks, bundles and suitcases. Squeezed in between were wounded Landsers, their filthy bandages hanging from heads, arms and legs.

A sailor, his temples already grey, approached and gently told me to follow him. 'Come along, boy, we've got some beds for you guys, down below. I'll give you a hand.'

He took my good arm and indicated that I follow him down the ladder which was some two metres high and vertical. No problem to climb this if you're fit and healthy, I thought, but how will I manage in my condition? Then I heard my sailor shout down the ladder. 'Jens!' he yelled to his mate, 'seeing as you're standing there with nothing to do, give this fellow a hand, will'ya, he's only got the one . . . We don't want him losing another.'

Next thing I knew, I found myself in my new abode, a cargo compartment where the ceiling reached down to about a centimetre above my head and a few bulbs shed a gloomy yellowish light. Looking around, I discovered three or four unoccupied bunks made out of wood, covered by the limp folding mattresses used for camping, a pillow in a blue-and-white check case and a grey woollen blanket. All the other beds were already occupied by wounded or sick civilians. There was a row of bunks lined up against each side of the hold and another row down the centre.

'Is that bed actually meant for me?' I asked Jens who was walking at my side. I could hardly believe my luck.

'Sure, as long as we have stock! Behind your raft there was another lifeboat, so there might be more coming our way. So, hop up, I'll help you. Your predecessor has sadly gone to a watery grave.'

All snuggled up underneath my blanket, I could hear the engines growing louder and the ship picking up speed.

Curious whether there was any medical help we could call on if necessary, I asked the Landser below me if he knew of any medics or nurses that might be on board. 'Surely not, that would be total luxury . . . but fear not . . . we'll soon be moved to an army hospital.'

'I'm exhausted,' I told him, 'I've come from the *Gustloff*.'

'Yup, we've heard . . . must have been absolutely dreadful.'

All I could tell him was that if anything even close to what happened with the *Gustloff* happened again, here with this freighter, it would spell our end. 'Nobody, nobody from down here below will ever see the light of day again. And unless I'm wrong,' I added, fully aware of the circumstances, 'there'll be no lifeboat for any of us . . . I've been through this once before.'

The Landser was more optimistic. 'Fiddlesticks, we've been assured of safe passage.'

'As for me,' I retorted, 'I'll only ever feel safe again when I feel firm ground under my feet.'

The Landser seemed to understand. 'Yup, I hear you, man, but frankly, I myself am happy as a clam to have escaped the pigsty at the front. I almost feel like I've already arrived home, safe and sound.

'Where's home?'

'Seesen am Harz', he answered, while my own thoughts travelled to my mother in Munich.

'What about yourself?'

'I'm from Munich,' I told him, now lost in thoughts. 'Not as safe as your place . . .'

The Landser was one of the hardy comrades. 'It'll all work out . . . The *Endsieg* is not far off.'

I wasn't quite sure what to make of his opinions and, as I didn't know the man, I decided to retreat into silence. It wasn't difficult to feign exhaustion. Meanwhile a soldier with his head swaddled in blood-soaked bandages was being stretched out in the bed to the left of me. The minute the sailors had put a blanket over him, he started wriggling and moaning in pain. 'Comrade,' he asked plaintively, lifting his eyes. 'D'you have a fag for me?'

'I'm really sorry, comrade, I haven't seen one in days.' I actually wasn't sorry at all seeing as the air in the cargo area, well beneath the water level, was so foul that we could well do without somebody smoking.

But, much to my annoyance, the guy on the same level at the far end had heard our newcomer's request and was more generous in spirit. 'I'll help you out, mate . . . though I've only got the two, here, take one! We'll be out of here soon anyway . . . D'you have a match?'

Snatching the cigarette, the injured soldier crumpled it up in his hand and sniggered. 'You lunatic!' the generous donor shouted, 'they sure got you damn good in the head!'

Our room was not heated, not designed to hold human freight and certainly not in such large numbers. The air gradually became so putrid that I could barely breathe. Some of the men spoke in their sleep, perhaps hallucinating due to fever. Turning and twisting their frames in tortuous convulsions, they'd cast their blankets off their burning bodies. I watched my breath condense in droplets clinging to the metal sheet roof above me. In some places water had collected and came plopping down in heavy drops. One such place was right above my head which meant that drops were landing right between my eyes. I was unable to fall asleep as I kept having to turn my head to avoid being incessantly splashed in the same spot and I became more distressed.

Desperately, I tried to figure out how long ago it had been that the voice on the loudspeaker had announced that it would be another three hours or so till we'd arrive at Swinemünde and be able to dock. Was that an hour ago, two hours?

Time was dragging. With every minute passing, I regretted more and more that I hadn't been put in one of the lower berths. Finally: 'We'll be docking in a few minutes at Swinemünde', not a moment too soon as I was suffocating with the stench.

It seemed forever until it was my turn. But the jostling and hustling which had broken out rather innocuously at first, when we anchored, now threatened to turn into the panicked stampeding I had witnessed, albeit semi-consciously, on the *Gustloff*. The still ambulatory wounded and civilians, alternately pushing and supporting each other, ruthlessly fought their way to the exit ramp. An eternity seemed to elapse before an elderly sailor approached my bed. Just as his comrade had done before, he slung my good arm over his shoulder and, with his other hand reaching out to the guy with the head shot lying motionless next to me, he mumbled: 'Ah, he's come to the finish line. We'll dispose of him later.'

Turning to me, he realised I was troubled. 'But that should not be your concern, boy,' he said to me in a friendly tone and took me to where the ladder hung. I found it quite difficult to climb up, fearfully clutching the first rung in my reach while trying to balance myself and at the same time heave my own weight upward. I failed, but suddenly saw a young sailor on his knees at the top exit reaching down and gripping my healthy arm to pull me safely up; a guy below helped by shoving me from behind. A few seconds later I staggered out onto the platform and what with the fresh air suddenly getting to me I faltered for a second and was about to hit the ground when two elderly men jumped to my side to support me. Once again I was reminded how astounding it is, what a battered body can overcome when a worthy goal is in sight. And it was. 'Come along, boy! Over there, it's only a hundred metres from the pier, there's a train waiting for you – it'll take you to the south!'

Just as soon as I was about to heave a sigh of relief, the sailor still at my side put on a damper. 'The train can only depart once it's dark,' he warned me, 'that's because of the low-flying aircraft buzzing around here. It's constant . . . During the day the smoke of the engine would attract the pilots' attention.' Nothing more needed to be said.

CHAPTER 9

To the Army Hospital

Just before boarding the train I was told to report to an elderly Red Cross Nurse. Positioned in matronly fashion behind a small table, she was busy officiously registering the passengers. Sitting on a chair in front of her, I watched as she wrote in capital letters my name, date of birth and rank onto a small hole-punched piece of cardboard through which was threaded a piece of string.

'There,' she grunted, tying it around my neck and, contented with her work, she praised herself, 'that's your profile now dangling on your chest. Gives everyone a chance to know who they're dealing with.' Turning around to her younger colleagues waiting in the back, she ordered them to help me onto the train. 'Give this comrade a hand, will you, seeing as he made an effort to defend our fatherland.'

I was grateful for the help and, trying not to groan too loudly, I dropped onto one of the wooden benches which were typical at the time for non-first-class passenger cars. 'Do you know when the train is scheduled to depart?' I asked one of the nurses.

'None of us know for sure,' she answered, a friendly twinkle in her eyes, 'but we do know that it'll be heading south, apparently to places where army hospitals have been set up. Good luck! Have a nice trip!' she waved and then turned her back.

Struck by the beauty of her face which reminded me of an angel, I wanted to keep the memory of this brief encounter in my head but then was jolted back to reality by my rumbling stomach. Several Red Cross nurses were passing through the wagon which in the meantime had completely filled up with wounded Landsers. Stopping in front of each soldier and greeted by loud heartfelt hellos, they poured lukewarm tea from large tin jugs into paper cups, which they handed to us along with a slice of bread spread with artificial honey. Not having seen or indeed tasted food since gulping down a few sips of tea and some rusk biscuits back on the ship of the East Prussian naval service, I realised that I was famished.

Some three to four hours went by before it finally turned dark outside. One of the 'chain dog' officers of the Feldgendarmerie passed through the corridors and, assisted by two of his flunkies, a pair of elderly sergeants, inspected each one of us from top to bottom. He took his sweet time. How smoothly things still seemed to be running in the rear areas as opposed to everywhere else, I thought cynically.

Legs spread wide apart, the officer must have decided that I was one to be interrogated. 'When and where exactly were you wounded?' he growled.

'24 January in Königsberg.'

'And how did you get out? How did you land up here? The Russians cut off the routes leading to this area! What's your explanation?' His tone was still abrasive and above all it was so loud that everyone could hear.

'From Pillau I first travelled on the *Wilhelm Gustloff** and was then switched to a cargo ship attached to the East Prussian naval service.'

The officer raised one of his eyebrows, clearly surprised, but his voice softened. 'Sure had a bit of luck, boy, speedy recovery!' he said, handed me back my paybook and turned to my neighbour.

Once the three chain dogs were out of earshot, the Landser diagonally opposite me with his hand in a sling could no longer hold back. 'You actually lived through that mess?' he asked incredulously, 'Or were you just having him on?'

'It's the absolute truth,' I answered quietly and when others quizzically turned their eyes on me, I felt strangely moved.

The train departed with a sharp lurch. 'D'you know our destination?' asked my neighbour, whose leg had been amputated.

'Nope, but what I gathered from the nurses and an old railwayman just before we left is that we're heading south, to some place where

---

* Hans's memory seems to be at fault here, perhaps because he had been so heavily sedated. His medical evacuation began in Pillau (modern Baltiysk), but he would have boarded the *Gustloff* in Gotenhafen (Gdynia).

there are army hospitals . . . and quite honestly I don't really care about the rest.'

It was pitch dark in our carriages to protect us from aerial attacks and the air was thick with cigarette smoke and reeked of cheap pipe tobacco. While at the beginning we engaged in excited chatter, it soon became quiet. Left to myself once again, my thoughts wandered to what I had been through, to my mother and to how lucky I was to have been given another shot at life. Was mother still living in Munich? Under the constant threat of being bombed? I recalled overhearing announcements made on the cargo ship mentioning enemy air raids on our city.

Convincing myself that surely my mother had been evacuated to her relatives in the countryside, I tried to stop worrying and eventually managed to fall asleep. But then came the dreams, images of the rescue boats which were nothing more than rafts in so many cases, the glacial sheet of the ocean, the howling, the freezing temperatures. And, again and again, I saw the *Gustloff* rolling, pitching and plunging to its watery grave. It all came flooding back – literally.

Bathed in sweat, I woke up. The train had stopped in a small town and a few Landsers hastened off – though some had to be carried.

An elderly Red Cross sister asked whether I too wanted to get off and stay there. 'We've got first-aiders on hand and they can take you to the army hospital.'

I asked her whether the train would continue further south. 'Yes,' she nodded, 'but whoever wants to remain here with us, can get off!'

I told her that I would stay put, as my intention was to get as close to Bavaria as I possibly could.

'Absolutely fine, young man! We're actually full up round here! Have a good trip!'

The train stopped at another place and a few more injured hobbled off the train. At the third stop the driver announced over the loudspeaker that it was the end of the line. 'This is Vacha. Last stop – everyone must now disembark!'

Carefully I stepped down and thankfully there were only about three steps leading down to the platform. Again, I was supported by a comrade, this time it was a lance-corporal who had been shot in the abdomen and grazed on the leg. 'Where's Vacha on the map?' I asked him.

'Why it's in Thuringia, not very far from Erfurt.' He wasn't too impressed by how little geography I knew. 'It couldn't have turned out better for me,' he enthused, 'it's so close to my home!'

'Sounds great for you, man, but for me it would have been much better if we'd gone just a bit further.'

'Fiddlesticks, just be happy that you're here. I couldn't help overhearing that you nearly went down . . .'

In the meantime, dawn had broken and in the first light of the morning we could see that the fields that bordered the train tracks were covered by a thin layer of snow. Our small group was told to board an ambulance and it took us right through the quaint little town, which had been fortunate to be spared by the war. Heiner finally introduced himself and it turned out he was some two years older than me.

We came to a stop at a large gabled building with a stone staircase leading to the entrance door. 'Well, look at this!' Heiner exclaimed theatrically, 'our *Gymnasium* has turned into an army hospital!' Chuckling, he added, 'Looks like I'll finally get to go to a decent school.'*

Laughter broke out expressing the relief we all felt for having had a lucky escape. The front line was turning into hell – we knew that much – and we no longer had to live through it.

Classrooms had been converted into wards and in the hallway, just by the entrance, a reception booth had been installed with a sergeant, one of his eyes covered by a patch, occupying the only seat. Sliding the screen to the side, he asked each of us to list our name and rank which he wrote down in his notebook.

'You two,' he pointed at me and Heiner, 'are allocated to room 3, over there, at the far side of the school's courtyard. Off with you!'

As we dragged ourselves painfully and slowly through the large rectangular yard we could tell from the numerous footprints in the

---

* *Gymnasium*, usually translated as 'high school', is the German term for a secondary school offering qualifications up to university entrance; Heiner may have attended a *Realschule* with a more limited curriculum.

snow that loads of soldiers must have already found refuge here. But with the yard also surrounded by barbed wire, the place reminded me of a prison rather than a refuge to convalesce in. 'Not really a warm welcome!' I complained to Heiner, who just scoffed.

'Hans, at least they don't shoot around here – and for me, that's the main thing. Methinks we will have no problem making ourselves comfortable here until the *Endsieg* – it's already February. And what spring has in store, well . . . let's wait and see. I can tell you one thing . . . I sure don't miss the old rifle rod.'

'Of course, Heiner,' I couldn't but agree with him and set aside my momentary despondency.

In the meantime, we had entered a long narrow hallway in the side building and stood in front of a door with the number 3 painted in black on it. Heiner knocked and we immediately heard a friendly voice inviting us in.

Had we been given the flat of a teacher's family? Only three beds. Brilliant, I thought. But then my glance fell on an officer's cap hanging from a hook on the back of the door. Turning my head a bit further and seeing a man of about thirty sitting in one of the three chairs beside an oval oak table by the window, I grew apprehensive. This would belong to him, I assumed, an officer, somebody not of my class. Dressed in long white and blue striped pyjamas he looked rather the well-to-do sort of man and his voice, a deep bass, complemented my impression of him.

'Why the long face, for goodness' sake?' he asked, amused. 'All I am is a dentist. That was the reason the Wehrmacht automatically pushed me up to officer rank.'

Taking a good long look at the two of us he then slapped his thigh, and assured us how relieved he was finally to have company in the room. Motioning with his head towards a cube-shaped radio, a Volksempfänger,* as we knew them from living rooms all over the Reich, he confided that he didn't think the broadcasts were very entertaining.

---

* Or People's Radio, a standard type of affordable radio set introduced by the Nazis and used to facilitate control of public information and propaganda.

'Just to clarify and so there's no misunderstanding,' he continued, obviously feeling awkward about the contrast between us two ordinary soldiers and himself, 'all I am is a simple dentist who just happened to be too slow getting from one spot to another and so I got shot. Chest wound.'

As per army drill, both Heiner and myself stood to attention, silent and listening to him with respect. 'Of course,' he chuckled, 'I get on famously with all the doctors around here, we're all on first-name terms. That will sure come in handy for you two as well. Do you play *Skat*?'

'Yes, lieutenant, sir,' shouted Heiner while I could only offer a meek 'A little'. 'But,' I added hastily 'I can pick it up very quickly. In Bavaria we tend to play *Schafkopf*.'

'That'll do nicely! Problem solved.' He shot a brief glance at his shiny silver watchband, pointed to a large cupboard next to his bed and asked whether one of us could help him into his coat. 'Over in the dining room they're serving breakfast,' he told us, 'army bread with substitute coffee, of course. The non-ambulatories get their meals served in bed, but anyone who can manage even as little as hobbling a few metres has to walk over under his own steam.'

What was once an assembly hall had been adapted to serve as a dining room. 'Sorry, guys,' our officer muttered on entering, and he sounded genuinely regretful, 'but I'll have to join those four at the corner table. It's the major sitting there whose abdominal injury still hasn't fully healed. He's a total bulldozer and can't wait to return to his battalion at the front. He even criticises the senior physician next to him when he feels that he doesn't discharge the men fast enough – he'd declare the poor sods *kv* [fit for war service] like a shot, pardon the expression. The other two are okay.' No sooner had he walked away than he turned round to deliver a last bit of information. 'By the way,' he confided, barely audible: 'tonight we'll be the first whom the senior doctor and his entourage will be visiting. He has to do his utmost to demonstrate that he's getting us lot ready to return to the front. But fear not, we are in good hands with this guy and his team.'

Then we were on our own. 'They sure landed us with quite an

oddball,' remarked Heiner, and I certainly felt likewise. 'But perhaps,' I thought out loud, intent on remaining optimistic, 'it'll turn out that we've lucked out with him.'

We then joined the Landsers who were sitting at a long table and warmly welcomed us. A rota had been set up with two of our lot on duty every third day to fetch the large coffee pots from the kitchen and then clear the table after the meal.

'Your turn tomorrow!' we were informed by a tall lanky guy who obviously delighted in assigning duties to others. His blue and white hospital gown flapping about his gaunt frame, he felt beholden to let us know where we stood in the pecking order. 'Let's put it to you bluntly, guys,' he declared in his thick Franconian accent, 'don't for a minute expect to get off scot-free and lounge about around here. This ain't no place to enjoy the blessings of our hospitality and shirk your fair share of the duties.'

Another boy, with a bright and softly pudgy face and a voice revealing his recent puberty, also wanted to show off. 'My oh my,' he squeaked, 'you're obviously the noble lot, living over there in the master suite while us poor sods are crammed in the main building ... But, no fancy coats for you, just wait and see ... the nursing assistants – all lovely-shaped birds, mind – will give you regular hospital gowns ... uniforms will be taken for cleaning.'

Yet another man, slightly greying at the temples, briefly looked us up and down and seemed content that we didn't have any extraordinary medals or party badges. His question betrayed a Hessian background. 'What area then was your hunting ground?' Conversation was in full swing, while Heiner and I enjoyed what we hadn't had for ages: breakfast under a roof, this one with a large Red Cross painted on it. Somewhat against my will, I actually started to feel at home in this place, though my wounds were becoming more noticeably painful.

An orderly handed us the obligatory striped pyjamas just in time for the medical rounds, and we were told not to take them off until we got more ambulatory and were permitted to go on outings. When it came to applying for these, we would have to submit a request form and receive a stamped permit at the door.

With amazement we noted how the senior medical officer greeted and dealt with our fancy roommate with genuine friendliness and had his two assistants, young medics, scurry around to remove the bandages from our lieutenant's torso. The image of the three doctors, dressed in brilliantly white coats from under which their polished army boots were peeping out, reminded us of a real hospital setting and the image was completed by three Red Cross nurses standing behind in readiness, next to an overloaded double-tiered cart on wheels.

While their backs were turned, we managed to catch bits of the senior medical officer's conversation. 'Tell me, Lothar,' he asked the lieutenant with reproach ringing in his voice. 'How on earth did you manage to get into this state? Your shot wound in the back had already nearly completely healed, and now this mess . . . inflamed again! Let's deal with this right here and now – or do you want to be sitting here for the *Endsieg*?'

Heiner and I were still standing erect next to our beds and couldn't hear the lieutenant's response. The chief then abruptly turned to me, ordering me to get myself into bed. 'Until I've finished with the lieutenant, just stay there. It'll be your turn next.'

'Remove the dressing,' I could hear the doctor instructing his team and then could only see two backs leaning over the lieutenant with the senior medical officer looking on, erect and stern yet now addressing Heiner.

'Had you had anything to eat before being shot?'

'No, sir, but I was certainly hungry.'

'You're sure in luck,' murmured the doctor all while looking at his notes. 'I can see that the bullet passed through your abdomen and didn't touch the intestines. We've had such cases, they've all survived and hopefully are still around today. But I can see that the entry wound is now inflamed and has ulcerated. Sister Erika!'

'Yes, *Herr Stabsarzt*?'

'Jot it down: list Lance-Corporal Heiner Rom for surgery, tomorrow morning. Cleansing of wound entry.' Turning to Heiner, he assured him that there was nothing to worry about.

'May I ask a question, *Herr Stabsarzt*?'

'Of course.'

'My mother serves as a midwife, right around here, at Geisa. She doesn't yet know that I'm here. May I call her before the operation?'

'Absolutely, once you have a bandage on, get yourself to the office, and call Geisa. Can't say we have a lot of mothers around here at present, but we know of their impact when it comes to patients healing more quickly.'

One of the young medics had in the meantime taken off the bandages from my left upper thigh, from my lower legs which had become infected due to being exposed to freezing temperatures, and from my right arm encrusted with blood. 'When they want to examine your abdomen,' he said in a low voice, 'you'll need to stand, but first up, it'll be your legs.'

The senior medical officer, now in front of me, showed little interest in my nose which had set, merely stating that it had been dealt with to a high standard. 'It's healing well, great job!' But looking at my other injuries he requested that I be scheduled for some x-rays. 'Quite possibly we'll find more shrapnel which our colleague at the front may well have overlooked,' he explained. 'That small piece of shrapnel,' he then dictated, 'is not of concern as it has been walled off on the inner side of the right arm. Keep under observation.' My poor legs didn't warrant his attention either, it seemed, but examining the newly inflamed area around the wound on my abdomen, he was less pleased and shook his head. 'Hmm, we'll get this sorted out as well, but it could take a while.'

The medical rounds took place daily, and though ours would never last as long as the first one, there was a palpable feeling of anxiety when the doctors moved from bed to bed. Quite a few of the comrades who had hoped for permission to remain at the hospital to recover more fully were handed a clean bill of health. That spelled a return to the dreaded front line, which was approaching dangerously close to us. For how many of these poor devils did this mean death?

Towards the end of February, we were told by our lieutenant comrade that as of the following morning the good major would no longer sit at his table. 'He's volunteered to go to the Eastern Front, would you believe it. He'll be so very missed,' he added sarcastically. 'Above all by our senior medical officer – the chief! Not for a moment did he let him out from under his gaze . . . kept peering over the poor chief's shoulders . . . Every medical decision that the chief took – it was just too lenient for this guy.'

We just laughed, secretly very relieved that so far, we had been allowed to stay put. While dreading being declared *kv* and forced to return to the front line, we did, by the same token, want to get sufficiently well to be granted an exit permit.

One day, when it seemed that a long time had passed since the start of our recuperation at the hospital, Heiner announced with a huge grin on his face that he had been given permission to visit his mother. 'Hans, this weekend I'm allowed to travel; I'll take the slow train to Geisa. And guess what, it's not just the once, but looks like I'll be able do this frequently from now on.'

Heiner was a decent fellow and he certainly knew to share. Before I could even respond, he announced that I too was welcome to join him on the outing. 'When mother was here last time, she took a liking to you,' Heiner began. 'Father is no longer with us . . . he fell on the Western Front and so now there's space in our small house. She'd love to cook for the two of us and she's got a knack.' You could see pride shining in his eyes. 'Hard times now, but farmers around the area often use her for this, that and the other, anything even vaguely to do with midwifery – and so she manages to get ingredients we can only dream of. So, how about it?'

'Thank you, Heiner. Not this time round. I've received an exit permit for this Saturday, so I'll take myself to town. Let's do it another time, please! I would love to come along!'

It was the beginning of March. My legs, nearly completely healed, had me walking short distances without too much pain. Enjoying the mild spring weather, I ambled through the streets and lanes and stopped in front of the display window of a general store. Since I needed some tobacco for my pipe, I entered the small shop where a few women at the counter were chatting loudly.

Vividly recalling an experience years before at the grocer's back home with my mother, I butted into the conversation, introducing myself with a firm '*Grüss Gott!*' greeting. A lieutenant, barely much older than me, suddenly took two or three sharp steps up to me, and with his right arm and straightened hand stretched forward at eye level, he barked: '*Heil Hitler!* Have you forgotten the German salute?'

'Indeed, lieutenant!' I responded, pulling myself up, extending my arm and calmly saying: '*Heil Hitler.*' I didn't shout.

'Your paybook!' His hand thrust forward, he grabbed it, wrote down my name and asked where I was stationed. A deathly silence had spread in the small store when the brash officer, a youngster like me, turned on his heels and left, not before turning around. 'This will have consequences!' he hissed at me and slammed the door behind him.

An intense discussion, more muddled and confused than angry, ensued among the few women. Meanwhile an elderly lady who seemed rather well-to-do gently pulled me to the side by my jacket sleeve: 'Don't worry, young chap, nothing awful is going to befall you. That conceited wind-bag lives right next door to our pharmacy. He's never been popular – not as a HJ-leader nor as a student at our high school. He's on leave just now.' Then, moving to the counter, she spoke to the shop-owner. 'Else, you know, don't you, that my husband and I don't smoke. Do be good enough to give this young soldier two boxes of cigarettes for our tobacco stamps, won't you? He has truly earned them, seeing as he greeted us so beautifully in his Bavarian tradition.'

I thanked her profusely and left the premises hurriedly, but as I stepped onto the pavement I nearly tripped up a young woman whom I knew from the surgery office at the hospital. Right from the start – but from afar – I had been attracted to her.

'Dearie me,' – her blue eyes twinkled, amused – 'I know your face! Aren't you the private who was spat out by the sea so that he could cause trouble round here?'

'That's me, all right!' I replied, and then, perhaps emboldened by the pharmacist's wife's support, hastily, maybe too hastily, asked her whether she knew of a coffee-house that wasn't too far away. 'Would you like to join me for a hot drink? Please say yes! It's on me.'

'Thank you, how kind! Yes, that would be lovely. Just two roads down, there's a small coffee shop at the corner. "Tante Frieda" often even serves real coffee or tea.'

With that, and as if it was the most natural thing in the world, she bent and lifted my arm, placed hers below mine since she was so much smaller than me, and we trotted off. A sweet feeling of sheer bliss streamed through my body. Hardly able to believe my good fortune, I revelled in the knowledge that such a charming and seemingly unattainable beauty was walking by my side. It was heaven. When she turned her face up towards me, I caught sight of a few locks of her blonde hair underneath her hand-knitted blue woollen cap.

The coffee shop, a small and cosy sort of place, was mostly filled with women and a few injured soldiers with whom I had a passing acquaintance. Quickly spotting an empty table at the window from which two ladies had just got up, I guided my pretty companion to the two seats. 'Is this your first outing? By the way, my name is Lisa.' Her voice was a very pleasant alto. 'Yes, exactly! My absolute first and I do beg your pardon that I haven't even introduced myself. I am Hans!'

'Of course – no need to tell me, as I know you from the doctor's notes,' she gaily commented and I was so pleased that she seemed the uncomplicated and cheerful sort.

'So, Herr Hans Fackler, and now would you like to tell me the story of how you escaped the sinking *Wilhelm Gustloff*, even though your legs suffered from frostbite and your good self was pumped full of shrapnel?'

'I'd rather not,' I replied softly.

'Oh, of course,' she didn't make it awkward, 'There are certainly more pleasant topics we can discuss. What did you have in mind for today? Something special?'

When I told her about my encounter with that stuck-up twerp, that conceited oaf who called himself a lieutenant, she burst out laughing so loud and hard that some guests turned around and Tante Frieda herself, dressed in her prim black uniform and little white apron who wanted to take our orders, merely stood waiting, moving her eyes quizzically from me to Lisa.

Still smiling, Lisa looked at the plump middle-aged woman. 'Tante Frieda! Might you still have some of your wonderful apple cake left for us and perhaps some coffee? That would be just wonderful.'

'You're in luck. You'll get my two last slices.' Tante Frieda was happy to oblige. 'I have plenty of apples, mind you . . . but flour . . . that's scarce goods these days. But I have my sources . . .' And before we knew it, she was telling us all about the *Herr Kreisleiter** who slipped her enough flour to bake his favourite pastries, seeing as he had such a sweet tooth. 'Ah yes, he likes to pop in here quite often, he does, to pick up his order!' Taken aback by her own indiscretion, she quickly put a finger across her lips and left us to it.

'Poor woman,' explained Lisa, 'her only son was a fighter pilot shot down somewhere over south Germany, and then, four weeks ago, her husband was killed on the Italian Front. But she's been quite remarkable, it's always been chin-up for this woman . . . she'd probably despair though, if she weren't able to spend time gossiping with her guests.'

We went back to chatting about more uplifting things and time went by much too quickly before I was due back at the hospital. On our way, we agreed to meet up again. We both hoped that perhaps we could try and catch up inside the school courtyard, rather than just leave it to chance encounters in the hospital. I was surprised at how detailed Lisa's knowledge was when it came to the farthest and tiniest corners of the two school buildings which we were soon approaching. Lisa accompanied me right up to the main building and seemed to enjoy the curious glances that others, also returning home, shot in her direction, while I myself couldn't hide my pride in having got myself what I assumed was a pretty certain catch. Quickly she slipped inside and joined her Red Cross colleagues in the room they all shared.

When I passed the office, the sergeant on duty deftly slid his little window to the side, calling out '*Heil Hitler!*' with a big smirk on his face. 'That'll have consequences!' he continued and informed me that everyone at the hospital was in the know, as the lieutenant had taken it on himself to come by and complain about my 'unsoldierly

---

* *Kreisleiter* or 'District Leader' was a senior Nazi Party rank.

behaviour'. My neglecting to greet a member of the Wehrmacht with the obligatory Nazi salute got me confined for three full weeks.

'Oh Lordie!' exclaimed my dentist roommate, much amused when he heard that I had been banned from going out. 'How stupid can one be! Of course, the senior medical officer had to take this decision – a pig-headed political animal like this lieutenant seems to be can cause our chief all kinds of problems.'

Even though I was ordered to do guard duty – despised by all – several times during those three weeks, the time went by much more pleasantly than I expected. Once, towards the end, some of my comrades told me about a textile factory in town which for some reason had to be shut down. Rumour had it that everyone was allowed free access and given permission to help himself to the plentiful stock which, however, dwindled rapidly once word got around.

Briefly debating how moral it was to take advantage of such an opportunity, I decided that if one did present itself to me, I would have a go and fill up my rucksack with some of these freebies. Who knows, I told myself, perhaps one of these days they'll come in handy. My conscience was put to rest when I observed most of my comrades 'organising' themselves in this way and such an opportunity did, indeed, come my way.

On the second day of my curfew while I sat in my room listening to the radio, Lisa managed to slip in. 'Listen, Hans!' she chuckled softly. 'I get to hear all kinds of things in my office, not all of it meant for my ears. I found out that your two roommates are out for the day and so I can come and pop in without having to worry.' Such coincidences came Lisa's way quite frequently and so, with her visits, the wait until it was time for me and Heiner to travel and see his mother went by quickly and indeed in a most agreeable fashion. In no way did I feel it was a punishment.

A few days before our departure I asked Heiner whether he would mind if I left my rucksack at his mother's place as I felt it was safer to do that than keep it in the hospital. Seeing as I had stocked up on sheets, underwear, shirts, towels and good-quality fabric, in short on everything that would one day turn out to be useful to start off my life after the war was over, I was minded to ensure that they were tucked away in a safe place. 'There's nothing left there in that factory,' I sheepishly admitted.

'Sure thing, Hans. I myself have already stashed away an impressive supply. Mother is dependable. Who knows to what use we might put these things after the *Endsieg*.'

I was fortunate to be able to accompany Heiner on several such journeys, thoroughly enjoying his home and his mother's warm welcome including her cooking. Towards the last week of April my shrapnel wounds had nearly completely healed, but relief was mixed with renewed anxiety. 'Sister Erika!' the senior medical officer on his rounds seemed stressed, 'make a note that Private Hans Fackler be put on the list with the others declared *kv*.' Deeply troubled by this ominous declaration I immediately envisioned being detailed to one of the motley army units which had been formed in desperation and arbitrarily deployed.

In the meantime it had become clear to me that all the talk about *Wunderwaffen* was nothing but pure invention for propaganda purposes and that each dead man, not just on our side, was one too many and that this so-called *Endkampf* was senseless. Would my good luck run out so shortly before the end?

Lisa was the completely reliable sort of friend. Not one hour had passed after the medical rounds were over than she waved for me to come out of my room. 'There's chaos in this building,' she whispered once she had motioned me to a quiet corner. 'We've never seen the likes of this before . . . But, today I managed to cross out your name from those declared *kv*. Nobody will notice, not even our good senior medical officer.' Hastily she added: 'The man is getting more anxious by the day. He's even delegated his medical rounds to someone younger . . . I don't know the chap. I'm getting the impression that everyone seems to be playing by his own rule book – doing everything possible just to avoid pressure from above.' Eyeing me closely, she realised how terrified I was. 'Peh, nobody'll notice that you are still around with all this confusion going on. The doctors are overstretched and there's constant coming and going. So, Hans . . . don't worry, we'll see each other a few more times!' And then she was gone, her work was calling.

Until today I have no idea how Lisa managed to cross out my name (though she didn't erase it) another three times from the *kv* list. 'Hans,' she once mentioned in confidence, 'don't fret, my colleague's doing the exact same thing and nobody has noticed. Don't lose your nerve!'

I didn't, and kept myself to myself with April nearing its end before I knew it. By good fortune I was able to 'organise' for myself a few packets of cigarettes since the owner of the store where I'd had my rather unpleasant *'Grüss Gott'* incident was favourably disposed towards me. These cigarettes were not purely for my enjoyment, but a useful bartering item. I exchanged them for a rucksack, some plimsolls, a pair of brown shorts and a white and red check shirt.

'Ahem,' commented our dentist nodding with approval, 'the young man is obviously thinking ahead. Nobody will ever suspect that there's a member of the Prussian Glory behind those civvies.'

By that time the Americans were rapidly approaching and it was surely only a matter of days until they reached us. The anxiety permeating not just our building, but the entire town which had largely been spared by the war, was tangible.

Then, one morning, just after having finished our meagre breakfast, another misfortune befell me. A young SS stormtrooper NCO, accompanied by a different medical officer, went from room to room and jotted down the name of each man who seemed even in moderately good health. While Heiner's abdomen had apparently not yet healed properly and the stormtrooper therefore had no interest in him, and since our good dentist was nowhere to be seen, I became the focus of this man's fury.

'Why the hell is someone like you still around?' he screamed for everyone to hear. He then yelled that we Germans had no intention of handing over Vacha to the Yanks without putting up a fight. 'Off, away with you. Our *Volkssturm** unit will make certain that we prevail!' Then, regurgitating the tedious refrain of how our *Wunderwaffen* would easily win the day and that the world would be

---

* The *Volkssturm* was a national militia raised in the final months of the war as part of Germany's last ditch defences. Many of its members were over- or under-age or otherwise unfit for ordinary military service.

left marvelling at how they literally worked wonders, he called on all in earshot to remain steadfast. 'And now – out!'

While he turned to hurry to the next ward, I managed to catch a glimpse of his lined face with nutcracker nose and chin. Shuddering, I felt I could do without this fool of a party fanatic whose recruits likely wouldn't stand a chance. Reluctantly I joined the motley crew of men already gathered in the school courtyard. Look at us lot, I mused cynically, what a sad bunch this wonderboy has selected to defend the town. A sergeant who had sat at my breakfast table that very morning – originally from Landshut, he had told me during a chat – whispered into my ear: 'As far as I'm concerned, this young lad can go screw himself. I'm off to visit my mother. Care to come?' I just nodded. 'It might be tricky,' he warned, 'but I've got my pistol on me just in case.'

Just as we were about to disappear, the SS NCO came into the yard. 'Report! Number off!'

This followed without a hitch. We were well trained. But the gung-ho officer seemed disappointed. 'What?' he exclaimed frowning, 'that's all? Only fifteen men who know something useful about the front line?' He obviously didn't feel that we were the confidence-inspiring squad he had hoped for but then, within a second, he'd gathered himself. Straightening his slender body he ordered us to vacate the yard. 'All of you – we're pulling out!'

At the exit two HJ boys, neither of them more than perhaps fifteen or sixteen years old, clad in their black winter uniform each with a rifle slung over his shoulder, stood waiting for us. Relatives of the *Volkssturm* clustered in groups on the pavement, gawking or gesticulating enthusiastically. I couldn't quite tell how many of them had volunteered, but they were mostly elderly and each wore a white armband around one of his coat sleeves. When mingled with hundreds of HJ youngsters, this was quite a sight. They didn't manage to impress me much, nor, as it turned out, my breakfast sergeant. 'Haven't clapped my eyes on such a bunch of heroes for a very long time!' he scoffed.

'Listen up everybody!' the young fanatic shouted in a voice accustomed to giving orders. 'You form the 1st Company of the 1st Battalion of the Vacha *Volkssturm*! I am your commander! We've been ordered to set up defence positions and anti-tank obstacles to the west of the town. Carts have already delivered all equipment to site. We've got a supply of anti-tank rifles, ammunition – the lot. Attention!'

Quite surprisingly all this ran smoothly. 'Forward, march!' And this too went according to the rule book, though I dare say that our marching column exuded anything but fitness for duty and readiness for action. The area assigned for constructing the trenches was admittedly well selected. A spade was pushed into my hands and away I toiled, in silence.

Towards lunchtime a horse pulling the familiar *Gulaschkanone* brought an urn filled with potato soup and because I, unlike the recruited civilians, still owned a complete mess kit, I was easily able to spoon the soup. By then it was lukewarm but still tasty.

After I had been digging away all afternoon, my lower right arm throbbed with excruciating pain and when I glanced down, it had swollen to double its size. I could barely hold the spade and happily had no other option than to show it to our company leader. Disgruntled, he sent me back to the hospital.

Another surprise was in store for me. The office at the entrance was empty. Scanning the doctors' office through the door which had been left ajar I could see the senior medical officer nervously giving orders to his medics.

Whether or not Lisa had purposely been waiting for me remains a mystery to me to this day. But there she was, rushing towards me on my way towards the lodgings and, hastily planting a kiss on my lips, she nervously whispered, 'Hans, tomorrow at the latest the Americans will be here! Let's hope the *Volkssturm* will just dissolve quietly and peacefully, so there'll be no unnecessary bloodshed. Be well! I'm staying here with the other nurses. We'll stick to our rooms and wait and see what happens.' Waving to me one last time, she left me standing there perplexed. How would the Yanks treat our women, I asked myself? They're not the Russians, but they're all soldiers, that much I knew.

Once I entered Room 3 of my building our dentist, sitting at his table, welcomed me with open arms, obviously delighted to see me.

'Well, thank the Lord I'm no longer alone. Heiner did the right thing. I wouldn't be surprised if he's already having tea in his mother's lounge. Let's just hope that the two of us get through tomorrow, as it'll be hit or miss, if you see what I mean.' Then, working himself up, he berated the SS man. 'Is he still acting like a damn fool? This could cause hell.'

'Not sure,' I replied honestly, 'but I get the impression that many will be escaping tonight. And frankly, I doubt that even the squad officer is as determined to fight as he makes himself out to be.'

'I rather hope he isn't,' said the dentist drily.

Pointing to a small chest next to his bed he changed the subject. 'The good old senior medical officer has given me that,' he remarked casually, once more his jovial self, 'and it is filled with fresh army bread, biscuits, rusk toast, hard sausages, some tins, three bottles of Mosel wine and a bottle of bubbly.' He seemed rather pleased. 'God only knows where he got this treasure from. I am all the more pleased that I don't have to eat it up all by myself . . . No,' he added resolutely, 'I'm sure as hell not going to leave this behind for the Yanks. And yes, I am certainly going to have a jolly good time this evening, in readiness for tomorrow's uncertain events.'

He followed my look as I worriedly studied my swollen arm, but didn't seem concerned. Advising that I keep it under cold running water as he knew that would help get the swelling down, he also thought that I should have a good wash. Seeing as we still had some soap left, he urged that I go about this quickly so we could indulge. 'Let's enjoy our meal while listening to the stories the *Volksempfänger* has cooked up for us. This too,' he concluded while preparing the table, 'will finish soon.'

It was an ample meal fully savoured by the two of us as if it was to be our last. We chatted until the wee hours and hoped that the SS sergeant with the big head wouldn't raise a stink the following morning and with any luck would leave us in peace and look out for his own safety. It was common knowledge that the way the Americans forged their way forward was by deploying their air force and artillery at the slightest obstacle. We were well aware that, rather than sacrificing any of their own soldiers, they much preferred to blast their way through cities and streets to gain access. We now simply had to look after ourselves. Towards midnight we fell asleep on a full stomach – and, myself, slightly tipsy as well.

The kitchen of the school-hospital was working and serving meals as it had done in the recent past, but because I wasn't hungry the next morning, I told my neighbour at table that he could have my ration. Palpable doom and gloom pervaded the dining hall and nobody dared speak in a normal tone of voice. Just once I caught the tail end of remarks from one of the men, who was clearly disgusted with the Sturmführer and, much like the dentist, feared that the guy was too trigger-happy when it came to his anti-tank weapons.

'Mark my words, the braggart is dying to bang away at the Yanks!' Told to pipe down, he didn't continue his rant. But apparently someone called Herbert had done a quick recce with his binoculars outside the city and reported back that he hadn't been able to spot anybody or anything, except for only a half-finished defence position.

Silence fell on the room again apart from the humming of an American reconnaissance plane. As the building my dentist and I had our lodgings in was a little way from the main block, we usually had a view of the courtyard only. Now, however, standing at the open window of the dining hall, we could see the street below us and, lo and behold, there was not a single German soldier to be seen. A few minutes later the intermittent rattling of engine noise intermixed with the screeching and grinding din of caterpillar tracks, punctuated by gunshots, broke the tension. And then we could clearly see them. Hulking down the street the first American Sherman tank rolled towards us, followed by another one and then another. American infantry soldiers, dressed in their brown battle uniform, moved cautiously behind, their guns at the ready, pointed in all directions. Stepping back from the window, I mumbled that the comfortable dining room was as good as any place to wait for the *Endsieg*.

'Quite right, Hans! It most certainly is an ending for all of us – today marks the collapse of Nazi delusions of grandeur.' Walking from our room, our dentist called out to all and sundry to make sure to leave their doors wide open. 'I've heard that the Yanks are nervous.'

'And for good reason,' replied someone. 'They've probably had some nasty experiences with these fanatics from the *Volkssturm* . . . not to mention this whole business with the *Werwolf*.'*

Some twenty minutes had passed when the entrance door was smashed open. A dark-skinned American kneeled at the threshold panning his rifle from side to side. A second one, also an African-American and armed with a heavy pistol, strode past him, scanned the area, leaned against the wall and waved the muzzle in all directions. He shouted something we couldn't understand back over his shoulder and a few from his squad came forward – one could barely hear the tread of their soft brown rubber-soled combat boots. Different from ours, I noted with curiosity, they reached only half-way up the leg and had laces.

Later a white, pale, lanky American with a short moustache curving around his mouth rested his body against our door frame and looked on as his comrade scoured our room. He lifted the lid of our chest next to the dentist's bed and found the empty wine bottle inside; disappointed he hurled it with such force through the air that it smashed against the wall with glass splinters flying everywhere. 'Where third man?' he asked in broken German with his steel helmet pushed so far back that I could clearly see his reddish blond hairline.

'With mummy,' said the dentist.

I had noticed quite a while ago that our conquerors kept chewing on something, sometimes nervously, sometimes with a placid air about them as cows chew their cud. Only later did I learn from the dentist that they were chewing gum. But all had one thing in common: each one of them eyed us suspiciously, sternly and with an unfriendly expression. Probably they thought of us all as 'Nazis'.

What struck me most was that not a single one of these soldiers seemed undernourished. Quite the opposite! Just then a well-rounded American entered, while tightly holding a pistol with an unusual long barrel. 'All coming with me! In big house place for you! We living here!' His German was understandable though also faulty.

---

* The name of a supposed Nazi resistance movement that would fight back against Allied occupiers.

With one last wistful glance at the lodgings which had served us so well until then, we obeyed. Within minutes all rooms had been vacated, though we were all permitted to gather our personal belongings and take them with us. We ambulatory ones crossed the courtyard in single file. Just before entering the back door to the main building we saw a stack of Hitler pictures piled up in a rubbish heap. Beforehand, none of us would have dared remove any of these pictures or rip off the Nazi flags and banners draping the building as this would have implied anti-German leanings severely punishable by the authorities. Perhaps the occupants had removed the Hitler portraits at the last minute and chucked them into the courtyard so that the Americans would not draw any adverse conclusions.

Hubert was a twenty-year-old hospital inmate from Room 6 and because of his head injury he often displayed erratic behaviour and talked rubbish. He most certainly was a liability. Passing by the images, he smiled child-like and lifted his hand obediently to the Hitler salute.

'Damned Nazi!' shouted an American standing close by and thumped Hubert with his rifle so violently on his back that it sent the poor dolt sinking to the ground groaning in pain. Our dentist stepped behind Hubert, lifted him up and, in perfect Oxford English, berated an American officer. 'Sir, the lad has suffered a head injury and often simply doesn't know what he's doing.'

'Walk!' shouted the GI, totally ignoring the dentist.

Once inside the main building we were told that an American doctor had teamed up with our medical officer to select those among us who were considered to be in good health. Only at that point did we actually fully realise quite how many of us the senior doctor had managed to keep at the hospital and thus save from returning to the front. As for me, I was in luck, as once again my arm had swollen up. 'What will happen to those selected?' I asked my neighbour, but he didn't know for sure. 'I overheard that they'll be taken to a prisoner-of-war camp in Hersfeld.

'It's been said that conditions are inhuman over there. Healthy comrades, it's rumoured, have been shipped out to the USA, apparently to be used as labour force. Or was it France?'

'And how do you know that for sure?' I queried, but he insisted that he had it from good sources.

As far as we were concerned, nothing much changed during the subsequent days and we were treated fairly. Why the Americans, our liberators, appeared to have no intention of advancing any deeper into the country was the only thing that puzzled us.

'What on earth is the matter with them?' was the exasperated question of the sergeant from Landshut with whom I had planned my escape. He then confided that he had cast away his good Luger, had 'flung it over the fence', he said, 'so that I don't accidentally get in the way of them making headway . . . and now? Looks like our feisty brethren from the USA are taking a little rest!'

I couldn't make sense of it either.

The building became increasingly quiet and the transports to Hersfeld rarer. But because the swelling on my arm had gone down quite considerably, our dentist sounded pessimistic. 'Hans, my lad, it might now actually turn out that you're next. As for me, looks like I'm still of no use. If you don't mind, let me have the honour of removing a last bit of shrapnel from your arm, if the senior doctor allows. Then, I swear, you'll be sure to have a wound and will have to remain here until it heals. But after that . . .' he sounded apologetic, 'well, that wound might heal quite quickly.'

I didn't hesitate for even a moment.

A few minutes later, Fritz (by then I was allowed to address the dentist by his first name) returned from the senior doctor's office with a big grin on his face. 'Hans,' he announced with delight, 'the guy has no objections . . . we can use his surgery. Yup, rules have sure relaxed around here . . . seems like nearly all the medics have done a runner. But, don't worry yourself, old chap, a dentist is also familiar with the human anatomy.' Turning around, he told me to hold tight and that he would look for someone who could induce sedation, as the anaesthetist had also disappeared.

Quickly he grabbed the person just passing by the sleeve. 'Weren't you a first-aider before?'

The man replied that he was and my dentist quickly briefed him. He wanted him to do nothing more than dull the pain of a minor incision. Fortunately, the paramedic agreed, cautioned me not to have anything to eat until the following morning and promised to return. 'Otherwise you won't be able to tolerate the ether,' he warned.

During the night I woke up twice, plagued by misgivings. Fritz, however, assured me that the procedure was nothing to worry about, as otherwise, so said Fritz, the medic would never have agreed. 'You must surely know yourself that all our medics from the front know their way around anaesthetics!' he added somewhat impatiently.

At 8 o'clock Fritz's assistant transported me into fairyland and by 9 o'clock I saw Fritz laughing down at me. 'Here you are again! The shrapnel got lodged between your ulna and radius; it must have been your thick gloves which stopped any further penetration,' he informed me and mentioned that he was rather enjoying this. 'Wasn't a big deal, really! The incision on your arm is now a bit longer than a professional would have done it, but, hey, let's forget about that. I didn't stint with bandages ... used everything there was ... so we have optimal visual presentation and the Yankee doctor will not select you.' He seemed quite in his element.

My anaesthetist in the meantime sat smoking in a corner of the deserted surgery with a dreamy look in his eyes. Clearly, we had provided him with some entertainment. When he heard Fritz admitting that he was planning to escape from there that same evening, his face became serious. 'Hans,' the dentist explained, turning to the two of us. 'I've got to do it, you see, because I fear that the Yanks will deport me. The remainder of the doctors will all do precisely the same thing, and frankly I don't really understand why the Yanks seem to have been turning a blind eye so far. I've got the low-down from the senior doctor. And your girlfriend,' continued Fritz, noticing my anxious expression, 'is a master at caring for recently wounded patients and I am sure she'll do an extra good job with you. She promised as much.'

My incision was, indeed, nothing major and healed quickly. But something niggled at me and it wasn't so much my physical discomfort, but the fact that we were prisoners and that the American guards made quite sure to remind us of this at every occasion. They would mostly sit around, two at a time, either in front of the building or on stools in the courtyard just next to the gate leading to the scrublands beyond. They would chat with each other and have a smoke. Twice, however, they fired a shot in our direction, up to our window because one of us inmates had, in their opinion, leaned out too far. When we ran in single file around the yard to take some fresh air, they would stand with their guns at the ready. They were suspicious of our every move. But that didn't prevent us – unbeknownst to them – from scraping away at the fence and cutting out enough of a hole to be able to crawl through at the most opportune moment. I was among the 'diggers' and am to this day grateful to those comrades, all barely able to walk, who provided cover while pretending to take a leak.

I can't deny the fact that the Americans had fun with us. Nonchalantly they would flick their cigarette butts into our path and I would often feel embarrassed for many of my comrades who scurried to pick them up and eagerly drew a last puff. Of course, I wouldn't have minded a smoke myself but refused to stoop so low as to allow these unfriendly GIs a spectacle of this kind.

CHAPTER 10

Escape or Russian Captivity?

On one of the first days in June Lisa brought me some news. 'Hans!' She seemed nervous. 'The day after tomorrow, or tomorrow even, this hospital is to be handed over to the Russians. The Americans apparently want to clear out of Thuringia. If', she took a deep breath, 'you really want to go for it – then you'd better do it now.'

'Lisa, thank you.' I was deeply grateful to her. 'In that case it'll have to be tonight. I cannot be caught out. But what about you?'

Lisa squeezed my hands long and hard and I could tell that she was holding back her tears. 'This afternoon I'm being given a ride by the American major in his Jeep. He'll be heading to Bavaria. But I want to wish you all the very best, dear Hans, and above all Godspeed. You'll certainly need it.' With a last wave she turned on her heels and quickly walked away. Well, I thought to myself, trying to keep calm, I suppose this is how it is. Immediately I set about putting my escape plan into action. I couldn't waste another moment.

There was no problem getting around inside the building. I swiftly put on my red-checked shirt, my brown shorts, the hand-knit lambswool socks and the plimsolls. A brief look in the mirror in my bedroom removed any apprehension I might have had. Nobody, I reassured myself, would imagine a Wehrmacht soldier behind these clothes. I hastily collected my washing and shaving stuff, my underwear and my shirt, and shoving it all in my bag. I recalled that the shirt was the last one I'd been able to put my hands on before the Americans had arrived at the textile factory. Taking the utmost care to remain calm and collected I strode out of the building, rucksack nonchalantly slung over my shoulder.

The high school also had a gym which led through to the courtyard but until then the door had always been locked. We patients had used it for exercise during our hospital stay and, when I arrived there, I bumped into a sergeant dressed much like me and animatedly conversing with the old caretaker. I could feel their eyes fixed on me as I walked up to them. 'Are you planning the same as me?' the sergeant asked, his voice lowered.

'Looks like it.'

'Did you get the news that tomorrow the hospital is being transferred to the Russians and they'll be taking over the whole of Thuringia?'

'Yes.'

'Where are you off to? By the way, I'm Franz.'

'I'm Hans. I'd like to get to Munich. But I've got no idea how I'll get out of here.'

He probably hadn't even quite heard what I had said but raised his voice in excitement. 'Guess what, I'm from Pocking bei Passau. Shall we do this together?'

'Excellent! But first, why don't you tell me how we can get out of here?'

This was the right moment for the kindly caretaker to butt in. 'I've got that covered,' he explained gently. 'Tonight at 11 o'clock I'll unlock this door for both of you. Not a problem. I just hope that it'll be sufficiently dark. And,' he obviously had this all figured out, 'should one of the two American guards on their stools not be asleep for a change, then you'll just have to cover for me and convince them that you stole the key from under my nose.' He then went on to brief us that he would leave the key in the door and wouldn't pick it up until we had both crawled through the fence. 'That shouldn't take you too long!'

I simply couldn't help myself but clasp the dear old man's hands and thank him profusely for his kindness. It then occurred to me that the senior doctor was no longer living in the building, and that I had seen hung on his office wall a rather detailed map of the region. Franz and I had already reached the corridor when I mentioned this to him and he immediately urged me to go and get it. 'Hans, man, fetch it right now. I've got a compass on me and between that and the map we'll manage to skirt the main roads, use footpaths, and with any luck we'll avoid the Yanks, or the Russians as the case may be.'

Since most of my comrades still in the hospital were not yet ambulatory I only bumped into one limping Landser on my way to the doctor's office. Looking at me slightly surprised, he quickly cottoned on and wished me good luck. The door to the surgery was unlocked. It took me just moments to get the map off the wall, fold it carefully and tuck it into my rucksack. It had what we needed, namely detailed information on Thuringia and its surroundings.

Not many were in on our escape plan, but the few who did know just wished us the very best, with two or three of them regretting the fact that they were too disabled to join us.

The caretaker was on time, waiting for us in the unlit gym hall. 'Unfortunately there's a bright moon shining,' he reported regretfully. 'I've watched the two guards for an hour already. At first I spotted the glimmer of cigarettes but there's been nothing of that for the past twenty minutes.' Not the optimal circumstances, we thought, but nothing we could do about it. 'Be on your way, lads, and best of luck. The door is open.' With a reassuring thump on our shoulders he warned us not to get caught. 'I'll keep my fingers crossed for you!'

Our first step outside, with our plimsolls crunching down onto the pebbled courtyard, seemed awfully loud what with the completely still summer night. Not the faintest wind. I was petrified. Franz seemed equally perturbed and without even giving each other a sign, we pressed ourselves flat on the ground. Should, despite our caretaker's assurances, the two guards not happen to be asleep, they'd have no problem spotting us straight away if we stayed on our feet. We both knew that ahead of us lay an approximately fifty-metre-long pebbled area which we had to cover undetected. We couldn't have been an easier target if we'd tried. As swiftly as possible, alternately tip-toeing and dragging ourselves on our elbows, we inched forward almost without a sound and I would marvel for a long time afterwards at how my companion managed this while carrying a small suitcase.

I didn't know whether the panting came from me or from Franz slithering next to me, but I was certain that it would not go unnoticed. I was bathed in perspiration, sweat pouring down from my face and burning my eyes. We knew, of course, that with the slightest rustle those guards would not hesitate to pull the trigger – and it was only at that moment that I fully realised what an enormous risk we had taken to escape the Americans and the Russians. But there was no turning back.

At long last we reached the narrow grass-covered strip with the barbed wire and were fortunate to land precisely at the spot where some days ago we had fiddled with about three metres of the wire mesh. As we lifted it slightly for Franz to crawl through, a soft rattling sound seemed to travel the length of the fence, but in the stillness of the night it sounded more like a loud ringing to me. Then it was my turn to shimmy through the gap but my rucksack got caught. With one swift motion of the hand Franz helped me out.

We had made it to the outside, but were nowhere near being safe. I could see Franz wiping the sweat from his forehead with one hand while carrying his suitcase with the other. Hurriedly, not wasting a second and without making a noise, we flitted between bushes and undergrowth, and after a few minutes dashing through the moonlit night we believed that we had finally made it beyond the guards' range of hearing and vision. Exhausted, we collapsed, our hearts thumping with a mixture of fear and exertion.

'Well done!' puffed Franz. I nodded. It took us at least ten minutes to gather ourselves. In whispers, we agreed to keep going, keep marching to put the danger zone behind us as fast as possible. The compass Franz had brought along was extremely useful, pointing us in the right direction. We wanted south. With each step, crossing neatly mowed meadows, then down a straight path through the woods, our anxiety levels decreased, allowing for more caution. Peering right and left, we darted through the landscape like wild animals.

It must have been about three o'clock in the morning when dawn broke and by then we had come across a lonely hut filled nearly up to the roof with fresh and beautifully fragrant hay. 'Seems made to order!' Franz chirped happily and agreeing heartily I dived right in.

'It sure wouldn't bother me if the Yanks didn't clear out of Thuringia just yet, so we don't get caught by the Russians,' mumbled Franz who by then could barely keep his eyes open.

Not faring much better, I mustered enough strength to respond and assured him that the distance to the Bavarian border wasn't huge and that apparently Bavaria lay within the American zone of occupation. 'Didn't you know that the Allies had agreed that they would divvy up Germany into four separate zones even before the war ended? Well, my dentist in Vacha was adamant about that. Can't tell you, though, how he had got his information.'

'He may well have secretly listened to the BBC,' mumbled Franz, half asleep.

Two, three minutes later Franz's regular breathing told me that he was no longer bothered by politics and I too nodded off. I woke up only because Franz had started moving about. The sun was already high and, poring over our map, we determined that it would only be some three kilometres further until we would reach a small hamlet, the name of which now escapes me. Actually, why remember it seeing as all the two of us wanted was to get home as fast as possible?

We could already make out the rooftops of some farms when we chanced upon two older women and a young girl who wanted to chat. The three of them were busy turning the hay with their rakes so that the sun could dry the grass from the other side as well. Many people like them still farmed in the traditional way; while haymaking machines such as tedders were about in 1945, they were not widely used. We could also see the crooked lines cut by the scythes.

They quickly gave us the information we were after. 'No Americans in our village. But there are a bunch in the hamlet next to us and this morning we heard that they're apparently about to decamp and let the Russians take over.' They were eager to find out if the two of us had more details but we just shrugged our shoulders. 'A friend of mine in Vacha,' I added, wanting to give them at least something to go by, 'mentioned that the Americans have agreed to leave Thuringia to the Russians.'

Sobbing loudly and therefore hard to understand, one of the older women grieved the disappearance of her husband and son. 'Both are prisoners of war in Russia. So . . . what'll happen if they now come here as well, what then?'

The other woman, more composed, spoke about what had befallen her menfolk. Her son was missing and her husband was soon to be released from an army hospital in Ulm. 'At long last, I won't have to ask my neighbour for favours once *Vater* is home again. It was impossible to manage on my own.'

The young girl seemed to have picked up what we were talking about and came up with the idea of us staying on for a bit and perhaps giving them a hand. 'Quite truthfully, we would love to oblige under different circumstances,' answered Franz for the two of us. 'But we're escaping the Americans and above all the Russians. Right now, we're on our way home to Bavaria and we're doing all we can to avoid them catching up with us.' We begged for forgiveness and hoped they understood. The woman who was waiting for the return of her husband immediately waved away any feeling of discomfort. 'No worries at all,' she said brightly, 'we're just about to make our way back to the village. Our daughter is cooking up a feast for us – an exception – we're having Thüringer dumplings and a pork roast.' She immediately invited us, explaining that the day before they had been busy slaughtering and though they had already shared part of the meat with some refugees they were housing, there was plenty left for all of us.

We were famished and gladly accepting the kind offer we also felt embarrassed that we strong lads were taking rather than giving. But we simply couldn't risk falling into the hands of the Russians or landing in an American POW camp.

Back on our way after having enjoyed a plentiful meal, Franz was both heartened by the progress we had made and optimistic about our prospects. 'If we stay off the main roads and go around occupied villages, we should, with a bit of luck, be able to make it home.' 'Absolutely,' I agreed. 'And if we're fortunate to bump into more people who are as helpful as these village folks, we stand an even better chance.'

We agreed that often it is the poorer people who are the generous ones and it looked as though at that time the wealthier folk weren't out and about. 'But my God, what a mess these Nazis have made of our country! Dreadful!' I said, angry at the misery the Nazis had landed us in. Franz took my point but remarked that surely ruining our country hadn't been their intention. 'Certainly, yes,' I agreed, 'but I still think they have plenty to answer for. Anyhow, now the war is over and, as usual, it's the rich man makes the mess and the small man clears up after him!'

Franz pointed his compass at a church steeple lying south-east, in a town, so we had been told, that was still occupied by the Americans. 'Let's walk around it,' advised my companion. That evening we realised that we had only managed to put twenty kilometres behind us and still had a long way before reaching the Bavarian boundary, but considering all the detours and not being able to walk on the major roads, we weren't too discouraged by this.

Throughout the following days we very much enjoyed the hospitality along with generous meals offered by the locals except for one horrid woman who shut the door in our faces. But never once did we have to spend a night sleeping in hay or straw and instead were always given a bed which had belonged to sons, fathers and brothers who hadn't yet returned or who had been killed.

I couldn't honestly tell you today how many days it took us to reach the Bavarian border.

It was a sunny summer's day when we came to an area spanning several fields and woods. Though we had double-checked with passers-by and locals whether it was safe to take that route, the place was now teeming with Americans. They had set up camp and surrounded the tents with tanks and other vehicles. There seemed to be hundreds of them.

'Damn!' I said with annoyance. 'How could we've known that there are masses of them here in Thuringia. But there must be a gap somewhere! Surely we can slip through during the night.'

Franz was totally demoralised. 'Here? Never! No chance in hell. We better take a short detour, perhaps just for a kilometre.' But suddenly he interrupted himself and with a wide grin pointed to an old man with hair white as snow, who sat up on the metal seat of a mowing machine which was pulled by a farm horse. Calls of 'Hüh-ha' encouraged the animal to quicken its pace. 'Seems to be a wealthy farmer,' noted Franz, 'and once he drives past here, we'll ask him for advice. And maybe he'll know a thing or two about leaky boundaries.

Ten minutes later we stood behind the mower, well out of sight of the Americans. The farmer's eyes seemed friendly and I put our difficulty to him. The old man scratched his head and pondered while scanning the American tents that bordered the field. GIs, all bare-chested, were playing baseball, or lying lazily in the sun.

'The field is actually part of my estate which is mostly over there,' he told us, nodding his head toward the other side of the space, to the larger of the two properties which we could see from where we stood. 'They've got no problem allowing me to farm my land.' Scrunching up his face and squinting, he focused on the spot where an armed American guard sat on a chair next to a path. 'Over there,' he told us, 'where the guy is sitting, right by the bridge leading over the river, that's where Bavaria begins. The guards change every two hours, which in fact will happen any minute now.'

Mischievously eyeing us from the side he told us the idea he had come up with. 'If the next guard sees the two of you working side by side with me in the field, he'll assume that we've all come out here together. You could well be my own sons.'

We didn't hesitate. I lunged for a rake and Franz took a fork and together we began loading the cart with freshly mown grass. We performed our task so eagerly that the old man told us to slow down. 'Not so fast – otherwise you'll finish too soon!' And at that moment, he spotted the guards changing. 'Look at that – like clockwork!'

About fifteen minutes later we hooked up the mower to the cart and were ready to leave. 'Does one of you know to handle a horse?' asked the old man.

Franz did and the farmer felt it best that he should take over. 'Lead the horse, I'll sit in the mower's seat and you,' he said pointing at me, 'can take that suitcase and rucksack and sit on top of the grass. Best make sure and tuck your stuff away – underneath the grass is good, just in case . . . But I've been watching him and it looks like the new guard is too lazy to get up. Boys, let's go!'

As hastily as I could I clambered up on the heap, the cart wasn't too full, and tensing up once again I stared ahead. The guard was leafing through some magazine, legs resting on a stool, gun leaning beside him against his chair. He barely raised his head and made every appearance of not wanting to be disturbed. A casual hand wave and we had passed through. Taking a deep breath, I knew that we had set foot on Bavarian ground.

Once at a good distance away from the border river, I heard Franz call back: 'Hans, that's gone swimmingly well!'

'If all borders could be crossed so easily, I sure would opt for the gypsy life!' I responded.

While the farmer was giving his horse food and water in the stable, Franz and I waited in the yard. 'I'll admit, lads, I felt a bit queasy ... wasn't a hundred per cent certain that the guard would be quite as sloppy at this job ... I'm guessing you don't have any discharge certificates.'

Not taking any notice of us shaking our heads, he continued ruminating about how the Americans could become quite fussy when they got their hands on the likes of us. 'Come on now, the two of you, follow me into the kitchen. Gudrun, my wife, will be happy to feed you.'

Walking ahead of us towards the imposing house, he turned around before pressing down the handle of the entrance door. 'I can only hope that my Herbert also meets people who'll help him on his return home.' Apparently, Herbert had been spotted alive when on his way back from Italy along with some of his comrades. That put him, the old man calculated, in North Tyrol by now. He had been given this assurance by a neighbour's boy who had just arrived home, we heard. 'We can only pray ... but discharge certificates are essential.'

Franz proffered a slew of reassuring words to our host, telling him that with so many families waiting for their sons to return, everyone was hospitable and opening their homes. In Tyrol as well.

'Where are you headed, boys?' asked the old man, wanting to focus on our lot. Franz explained that I wanted to get to Munich while his family lived in Pocking. Describing the route we had envisioned, he explained that we wanted to avoid Bamberg or Nuremberg, seeing as we didn't fancy spending time with the Americans. We were going to part company somewhere in the Altmühltal and then make our own way.

'Quite a journey ahead of you,' admitted our host but then ushered us into the kitchen.

An hour later, with a full stomach, we were on the road once again. Franz's feeling was that the reason we had been so lucky until then was because the Americans were still new at this game but that we would need to be much more conscious of not having official discharge certificates. I couldn't have agreed more. The idea of ending up in a prisoner-of-war camp was horrific to my mind and even more so the possibility that the Americans could ship me over to the USA.

We forged ahead, cautiously, apprehensively, hiding like hunted animals and cutting across the hilly landscape, over rivers and across valleys, direction south. Often, well camouflaged, we'd lie pressed to the ground and observe American Jeeps on their patrols hurtling along side streets whirling up dust trails behind them. At times we would hear GIs making loud remarks about young girls or women working the fields and sometimes they stopped to flirt outright. We remained undetected and took care only to ask for directions when the air was clear. People were generally happy to assist.

Even though we would frequently have to resort to lengthy detours or remain under cover somewhere in the undergrowth or in a wood to avoid being spotted by the guards at a checkpoint, we gradually made headway towards home. The kind gestures towards us *Heimkehrer** were, with barely an exception, offered liberally and touched us deeply. Not once did we have to spend the night under the stars and we never went hungry.

We had already traversed the Hassberge, intending to bypass Bamberg, when we thought to ask a simple farmer and his wife toiling away in their grassland if it was safe to cross a bridge over the River Main. It was a good move, as the couple emphatically warned us against doing so, pointing out that the bridge we had in mind was heavily guarded by the Americans. 'No way, you can chance that and

---

* *Heimkehrer* = 'homeward-bounders'.

beware, lads, the town itself is teeming with Yanks – you certainly don't want to bump into them.'

Naturally, we followed their advice and instead chose a field path running alongside the riverbank while looking out for a suitable spot from which we could swim across. Deliberating which route to take, we saw a Jeep slowly driving towards us. There was no escaping. Without a further thought, we tore off our clothes, dived into the marshy bit of the river and splashing around pretended to be harmless boys taking a swim.

The Jeep stopped, the Americans even called out something, but when we didn't react they just drove off laughing. 'Phew, we just about scraped by,' admitted Franz. We were relieved.

A quarter of an hour later we had arrived at what we considered the right part of the Main for our swim across. Hidden from unwanted looks, we changed behind a bush.

Again, Franz brimmed with optimism. 'Dead easy!' he shouted up at me while I was still busy shouldering my rucksack with my few belongings and clothes stuffed inside. Franz held his small suitcase on his chest and did the backstroke, all the while laughing and boasting about his vigorous flutter kick.

On the other side of the riverbank we didn't bother with clothes but just ran quickly on for a bit wearing only our plimsolls. 'Let's get away as fast as we can!' I hissed. 'If one of those gum-chewing twits discovers us, there's no way we can run as fast as he can shoot.'

'I have no idea why these GIs seem so anxious – what are they afraid of?' wondered Franz and answered his own question. 'Maybe they've had bad experiences with us lot.'

Stumbling over a railroad embankment we reached a wood and only then did we take a moment to catch our breath and slip into our clothes. Whatever might have got soggy and wet during our river crossing dried in the hot June sun. That night, as in the past, we were fortunate to find shelter and be offered some food.

Our journey continued with the two of us continuously on the look-out for hotspots that needed avoiding. We went around Bamberg and two days later we arrived in the Franconian Switzerland district, north of Nuremberg. I am not sure what had got into us, perhaps it was the beautiful landscape luring us lads into believing we were on a hike, but we took it easy. Blithely, as if without a worry in the world, we picked berries in the woods or, when passing underneath cherry trees, treated ourselves to the delicious fruit growing in full bunches on the branches. Chatting and laughing, we actually enjoyed ourselves. 'Hans, even nature is looking out for us!'

Before I could even comment, an angry voice cut through our reverie. 'You rascals! Don't you have better things to do than steal my cherries?'

Mortified, we apologised and because Franz managed one of his boyish smiles the grey-haired farmer calmed down. He wanted to know who we were and where we had come from and after we told him our story he turned out to be quite amiable. As so often, by evening time we were sitting at his kitchen table having supper. Apologising for what she deemed meagre offerings, the farmer's wife – as had happened so often before – confided in us that she was feeding quite a few refugees whom they were sheltering.

Husband and wife would have liked us to furnish them with more information than we actually had. As so often during our journey, this conversation made it painfully clear to us how our once proud Germany had been decimated, destroyed and cut up by the war. Would we ever have believed two years ago that we soldiers would be reduced to furtively sneaking our way back home?

A thunderstorm surprised us the following day. Finding shelter underneath the awning of a small deserted cabin, we declared contentedly that we had made good progress, though both of us were soaked to the skin . . . We had reached the Nuremberg Reichswald, south of the city, which we had succeeded in bypassing.

Satisfied, we nevertheless didn't lose focus and remained on guard. My concern was what would happen to me once I was on my own. 'Hans, stop fretting. If neither of us gets ahead of himself, we'll both make it home safely.' 'After we split up in the Jura, you'll be taking the route along the Danube,' I said to Franz and I felt queasy even at the thought. The two of us had got used to each other and we got on well. Franz cajoled me out of my bad mood. 'You'll do well – you've got it figured out.'

Two days later Franz and I parted company, just near Greding, some thirty kilometres south of Nuremberg. I decided to walk along the highway but kept my ear out for any engine noise in case American vehicles were coming close. The second I heard the faintest rumbling I hopped behind the closest shrubbery. At that time, the beginning of June 1945, only cars belonging to the victorious Allies were seen on the *Reichsautobahn*.

After Greding the highway winds through the Altmühlpart and then upwards through the Jura. I knew that once I reached the top where the highway continues across open terrain, I would have to resort to side roads. But it didn't come to that. Suddenly I heard engine noise and I swiftly hid in a passing place slightly off the highway. I couldn't believe my eyes: a Wehrmacht truck with the familiar camouflage colours of a green basecoat with a hard-edge pattern of dark yellow and red-brown stopped some ten metres away from my hide-out. 'Erwin,' said one of the guys, 'don't be like that! The Yanks aren't in a hurry . . . we'll deliver the stuff to them when it suits us. Still can't figure out why they'd hire us for lugging their cargo without guarding us.'

I couldn't quite catch what the driver shouted down from his cabin, but I got up and walked up to the Landsers who, dressed in drab uniforms, stared at me in disbelief. The white letters PW were clearly marked on the backs of their tunics. 'Where are you headed?' I enquired boldly. 'Might there be room for this wretched tramp?'

'Sorry, mate!' the obviously most senior of the group responded from behind the steering wheel. 'It's much too tight here in this cabin already.' Justifying their voluntarily working for the Yanks, he pointed out the quality of the food they were enjoying courtesy of the Americans and the fact that they couldn't return to their homeland as the Russians occupied it. 'The cargo area is full to the brim with some weird electrical machinery. Sorry, matey, really sorry . . .'

In the meantime one of the other men, who had just relieved himself, loudly interjected. 'Erwin, for God's sake, how can you leave the guy standing here? Why, just let him sit on top of the roof! There's no way we can drive fast with this old rattle-trap.'

Gripping a handle I hoisted myself up and half leaned back ready for the ride. Our destination, they told me, was the SS barracks in Munich which had apparently been taken over by the Americans. 'That's fine by me,' I called down but asked that they drop me off well before arrival. I certainly had no interest in meeting up with their bosses.

'We kind of assumed you'd want that, pal!'

From atop the truck I enjoyed a splendid view of my surroundings. After a few kilometres, we rounded a long bend in the road and I got the shock of my life. Some few hundred metres ahead of us, American vehicles were parked and blocking off the road with military police busying themselves around them. Hand-painted white circles, broken up by the MP insignia, marked their helmets.

Our driver slowed down and as we approached the checkpoint one of the three hung his head out of the window and turning his face upwards to me insisted I need not fret. 'We've got good papers and as of now you're one of the team – you're looking after the cargo.'

Two of the three military policemen stood casually leaning against their vehicles, and only a lieutenant strode towards us. Taking long measured steps he approached the driver's window, raised his eyebrows and stretched out his hand. In near-perfect German he requested the driver's papers: *'Ihre Papiere, bitte.'* Obviously impressed by our driver's prompt response, he only cast a fleeting glance at me atop. 'And what about the young man in civvies – also belongs to you?'

'Yes, sir, he is the technician in our shop. He actually only looks young, but he's responsible for the cargo, he is!'

Tipping his helmet with his forefinger, the lieutenant told us we could drive on. *'Sie können weiterfahren.'*

As our relatively shabby vehicle passed the considerably larger American army truck, I wondered what sort of papers had so impressed this lieutenant. But brushing aside away any further speculation, I felt it best to let it be. I had learned by now that if something worked, no more questions needed to be asked.

At the following two checkpoints our papers worked in the same way.

We had nearly reached the SS barracks when I thought it best to hop off and make my own way. I was elated. Never had I allowed myself to believe that I would be able to reach home so quickly. Then, after thanking the comrades who had helped me so willingly, my initial euphoria evaporated.

I was brought down to earth by the sight of the city, large parts of which had been flattened, buildings bombed into rubble, I felt alone and deeply troubled. I barely recognised my home town. Walking carefully through a broken landscape to reach my home at Robert Koch Strasse 14, I knew that this next bit of my journey was going to be tricky. I prayed that our apartment block had remained intact and that my mother was alive and well.

CHAPTER 11

What Now, Hans?

Careful to dodge any approaching American Jeeps, I picked my way through the ruins of Munich. It was a miracle that I wasn't stopped. The curfew imposed by the occupying power prohibited lingering in the streets and so I quickened my step along the narrow pathways – the main roads had only been repaired inadequately – and bypassed buildings bombed into rubble and homes reduced to an uninhabitable mess of glass. The neighbourhood, once so familiar to me, was now alien. With every step I took, I grew more anxious as most dwellings had been destroyed and the heaps of ashes and debris that remained left me fearful of what number 14 would be like once I arrived at my street.

I still didn't own a watch, but estimated that on that day, 23 June – it is still etched in my mind – it must have been 5 o'clock when I stood in front of a large mound of rubble that had once been the house where our apartment had been. Was mother still alive? I knew that Frau Schätzl, one of her friends, lived in Sternstrasse, a nearby street. I'd go there straight away, I decided. She would surely know what had happened to my mother.

Looking both ways to ensure the coast was clear, I began to run. A few minutes later I knocked on the door of the ground-floor flat in an apartment block that had miraculously remained unharmed. Frau Schätzl opened the door and, first staring at me in near disbelief, her worn face then broke into a wide smile. Briefly she embraced me, calling back over her shoulder to her husband. 'Sepp! Hans is here! You know who I mean . . . Klara's son, the boy we all thought we had lost. Klara, my friend!'

She pulled me into the living room and couldn't get the words out fast enough. 'Your mother is alive! She's living with friends in

Lichtenweg – a hamlet of some four or five farmsteads in Isen. But there is no way you can travel to the countryside tonight. That would be much too dangerous.' Frau Schätzl then explained that while her flat was fully occupied, sheltering fugitives who had been bombed out of their homes and refugees, who were now sleeping in their living room, she could offer their kitchen for me to sleep in. 'You can use the sofa. Tomorrow, between ten and twelve noon, we're allowed out to get food. After that, you're good to make your way to Lichtenweg.'

Based on my letters, mother had known that I had been sick and was recuperating in the Vacha army hospital. But since the end of the war the postal services hadn't been working and, not having heard from me any more, she suspected that I had ended up being taken a prisoner of war by the Russians. So she was overjoyed when, on 24 June, after a long march on foot, I stood there on the threshold of the farmhouse.

Lichtenweg was a tiny hamlet and for a while I would be the only young man living there along with my mother, two women friends and the ten-year-old daughter of one of them. No sooner was the initial excitement over than my mother started to worry. 'Boy, do you have your discharge certificate?'

I admitted that, regretfully, I didn't. I explained, 'I had to run away from Vacha to escape the Russians. Otherwise they would've kept me there, you see.'

Not to be left out, the mother of the young girl butted into our conversion and immediately urged me to stay on with them all. 'No problem, Hans, you can live and work with us, and while we don't have much, we have enough to spare that nobody need go hungry. But', she added, lifting her forefinger, 'tomorrow you must go to the mayor and register.'

My mother was overjoyed when she saw that I was happy to remain with them.

The Isen mayor turned out to be not just a solid farmer but an upright and helpful human being. At first, on hearing that I didn't have an Army discharge certificate, he raised his eyes in suspicion, enquiring whether I had belonged to the SS. 'No, sir, I was a private serving with the pioneers.'

'Much better, young man. However, when it comes to handing out food stamps, I'll only be able to do so once you can submit a discharge certificate.' He assumed that I was well aware of rationing and that food could only be purchased based on stamps. This got me slightly annoyed as how on earth was I to conjure up such a certificate. The mayor asked me to compose myself. 'Strength, my boy, lies in remaining calm and collected. Looks to me like there are no skeletons in your cupboard, right, and you've only served two years as a soldier. We've got a prisoner-of-war camp in Erding, and though it's not the cosiest of places, I do know that they've already discharged two respectable young men, and you seem to be a similar candidate.' I wasn't quite sure where this was going, but he continued unperturbed, leading up to some sort of solution, I gathered. 'What these two guys did was report to the prisoner-of-war camp and two days later they left holding one of these desirable pieces of paper in their hands. They were simply Landsers – that's all.'

Briefly reflecting on what to suggest further, he mentioned that he knew my mother. Then he told me that he would lend me his bike with which I could travel to Erding, store the bike with one of the farmers with whom he was friendly and leave it there until the Yanks had released me. 'If you're lucky, boy, then you could be back in three or four days.' Gazing searchingly at me, he wondered whether I still had my paybook which luckily I still did.

'Any heroic activities noted in there? Any medals you received, any decorations?'

'No, sir, only my injuries,' I replied grinning.

Rising from his chair he asked me to follow him out of the kitchen which doubled as his office and to his shed from where he fetched a Wanderer bike. 'Look after it, it's my treasure!' he emphasised while wheeling it towards me. 'These beauties have become quite expensive these days and often get stolen.' He wasn't finished. 'And I want to say something else. It would be good if you went to the camp carrying some food. I've been briefed by the two lads. Yes, the Yanks have plenty of food for themselves, but they don't like sharing with Nazis.' And with that, he wished me luck saying he hoped to see me soon.

The prisoner-of-war camp on the outskirts of Erding was heavily guarded and surrounded by a tall wire-netting fence. Looking closely I could make out a large number of grey-clad men lying on the ground; there were no badges on their shirts. It certainly didn't look in the least bit inviting. In among the grey figures, I spotted just a very few tents and all I could think of was the weather, hoping that it wouldn't rain during my stay at that place.

The two GIs at the gate seemed more interested in the contents of my small burlap bag than in my paybook. While one of them fingered my hard-boiled eggs, a piece of smoked meat and the round loaf of home-baked farmer's bread, the other one stood behind me menacingly, his gun at the ready. Only after that did one guard briefly glance at my paybook and I doubted whether he could even make out what it said. Turning his head with a nod over his shoulder he indicated I should get myself to the barracks just outside the fence where several Jeeps were parked and a floppy American flag dangled from a high pole.

It was warm and sunny and I could only pray for the good weather to last over the following few days. With a bit of luck the mayor would be proven right and my imprisonment would not last long. At the same time I was plagued by worries of what might happen to me if it didn't go to plan. What if I was forced to stay here? Might I be shipped overseas? While I was deeply perturbed I was also conscious of the fact that without a discharge certificate, life in freedom was not a possibility. I knocked at the door of the barracks.

'*Grüss Gott!*' I said firmly on entering. An American officer leaning back in his chair behind his desk examined me without saying a word, and didn't greet me in return. After some three, four seconds he asked me in perfect German whether the paybook I was holding belonged to me and where I had left my uniform.

'Yes, this is my paybook and I left my uniform in Thuringia. I escaped Vacha, prior to the Russians taking over the army hospital I was in. You see me now in exactly the clothes I wore walking to Munich.' Without pausing, I immediately asked whether I could get a discharge certificate from them.

'Show me your paybook! Were you attached to the SS?'

'No! I was in the pioneers and only on the Eastern Front!'

'Well, let me see for myself.'

While he was leafing through my service record book I thought that I detected a particular German accent which reminded me of the Berlin dialect that some of my comrades had spoken. I suspected that perhaps this the officer sitting before me was a Jew who had been forced to flee from the Nazis. Before I could even finish my thought, he lifted his head sharply and demanded: 'What, your nose was also injured? Let's see!'

He studied my profile closely, placed my paybook on his desk, thumped it with his palm and then told me, albeit somewhat friendlier, that they would look into this further. 'That can take a few days. And only once we can be certain that we haven't come across any incriminating evidence against you, we'll discharge you. Your paybook remains here! Report to my office if you hear your name called out on the loudspeaker.' Pointing to the door he quietly added: 'Just find a spot for yourself.'

Just before reaching the door, I heard him asking what I was carrying in my burlap bag. 'My mother has been bombed out and is living with a farmer in the countryside. She was able to put some rations aside for me.'

'Aha, and now off with you!'

It was surely thanks to the extra food I had on me that two ex-tank soldiers took me into their tent. What was it? Were the Americans not expecting so many prisoners or were they just assuming that all of us young soldiers were Nazis who didn't expect better treatment? The thin soup and the square tin-shaped white bread distributed only twice during my stay were barely adequate for us not to die of malnutrition. What a relief it was to hear my name called out on the loudspeaker on the afternoon of the third day.

The same officer who had interrogated me on my arrival handed me my discharge certificate but vigorously shook his head when I requested my paybook. 'That'll be put into our files. Just be happy that you've made it out of here!'

Certainly, the discharge certificate was more important to me than proof of my military career and I took my leave. Facing once again the dreaded checkpoint, my mind was at ease this time round and pushing on the bike pedals I even felt cheerful. The guards ignored my exit.

After I returned the bike to my benefactor, he simply pressed a stack of food stamps into my hand. 'The woman with whom your mother is lodging will be well pleased to have a man staying with them. Her husband has been put to work at a mine in France.'

Mother had to toil away out in the fields, and though I was grateful that Lichtenweg had offered me a roof over my head, nothing, I realised, came for free. While I, of course, understood the circumstances, I simply hadn't been born a farmer's son and my dream was to work in my trade in the city. Despite mother's protestations, and the other women's regret, she organised a battered old bike for me with which I took myself to Munich. Not unexpectedly, the chain snapped just when I had reached Waldtrudering, a district on the outskirts of the city. Cursing, I pushed my two-wheeler through the streets, heading for my Uncle Karl's place – he owned a construction business that had survived the war.

Embracing him, I was profoundly moved when I realised how genuinely happy this elderly man and his family were to see me and gratified that I had found my way to them. That whole evening was spent exchanging stories and memories, but I knew that I didn't really wish to work in the firm of a relative. The following morning, I quickly repaired the bike and cycled to Robert Koch Strasse. I had applied to, and been accepted by, the Kolping Association,* who would provide me with a room in one of the homes they owned, provided I became a member or, as they called it, a Kolping son.

While I put myself down to work as a joiner, my plans didn't pan out. My former employer had been killed in the war, and though his previous shop, bombed by the Allies, had by then been restored, my job application came to nought. 'I would love to hire you, Fackler,' said the new manager shaking his head in regret, 'and, by God, I've got more than enough orders . . . but sadly I simply can't get my hands on enough decent quality wood.'

---

* The Kolping Association is a Roman Catholic organisation that was originally established to assist young working men.

Refusing to be defeated, I made my way to the employment office in the Implerstrasse. Climbing through lifted concrete slabs and shattered glass I found the entrance door to the building, which had also been badly damaged by the air raids. With the windows provisionally blocked off by coarse planks of ply poorly nailed to the frames, the corridors were only dimly lit. Though paper was also a scarce commodity at the time, I marvelled that this didn't seem to impact on the bureaucracy as I filled in page after page of a questionnaire. A thin man, with one sleeve empty and tucked into the pocket of his threadbare overall jacket, his temples greying, hovered, standing then sitting, behind his simple desk made out of spruce. But lo and behold, he came up with the goods. 'I've got something suitable for you, young man! BAGDi [Backofen & Dietz] are looking to hire an in-house carpenter, and frankly, I couldn't think of anything that would be more appropriate for you, looking at your background.' He then added that the firm was known to treat their employees well, 'They don't just pay the Reichsmark but offer benefits. Find out for yourself,' he advised and sent me on my way.

That evening I returned to my lodgings happy and content. As a Kolping son I paid little for my room, and half-board with breakfast and supper only cost 1.50 Reichsmarks. The Kolping house, an old building, was full to the brim. Not a single bed remained empty. While our meals naturally were terribly simple, they were nourishing and often we lads would ask ourselves how the good sisters managed to procure bread, potatoes, butter, eggs, vegetables and suchlike. Though quite honestly, as long as none of us went hungry, we didn't much care.

And as for my new job, I couldn't have struck it luckier, as the firm's canteens provided free daily lunches, very tasty ones at that, as part of our salary package and that included Saturday as at the time it was a working day of course. Additionally, every employee received ten cigarettes daily. Because you couldn't easily buy cigarettes in those post-war years with Reichsmarks that had become virtually worthless once again, this served me well as I could barter for products that were in short supply such as butter and coffee. The black market was booming and not only in Munich but everywhere in our now impoverished Germany, and cigarettes were effectively a recognised form of currency.

As happens so often, the poor were the losers in this respect as well, as they had next to nothing they could exchange for food. Turning my head in shame to the pavement when I passed citizens who stared out at me with a hungry look in their eyes, I felt awful and powerless, unable to help them, especially when it came to children. It was sadly true that the two years I had spent in the war had hardened me. On the other hand, I had to remind myself how long, after the sinking of the *Gustloff*, it had taken even me to have a joke with people.

Out walking on a Sunday morning, I bumped into my old friend Gerhard Hugel. His home, too, had been bombed into rubble and so neither one of us had found out what had happened to the other. Gerhard was the HJ youngster who had responded so many years ago to the recruiting officer's query as to whether he would sign up for the *Hermann Göring* Division, with the impudent words that he would like to think about it.

We were thrilled to meet again. Throughout the war he'd worked in the air defences, overseeing an anti-aircraft gun department, and he realised, of course, that he had fared better than I had. 'But,' he added, 'believe you me, I wasn't licking honey either . . . I'm doing great now, as I've got a job with the Yanks. I'm a kitchen assistant and making a good salary.' He then asked what I was up to and I told him that I had found work with the BAGDi firm and was living in the Kolping home and having to pay very little for this privilege.

Gerhard had a hard time understanding why I would voluntarily sign up for a place where the nuns running it were notoriously strict. 'Are you serious?' he asked in disbelief, 'You're actually submitting yourself to those penguins? Wouldn't be something to my taste . . .'

'Not mine either,' I retorted but didn't want him to think ill of the nuns who were bar none very generous towards us. 'Those penguins, as you call them, aren't nearly as bad as you think. I'm really grateful for their support at this time, but yes, eventually I'd love to find a place where I can be a bit more free.' I asked him whether he would join me on my walk to the Isar. 'Remember when we played around the Maximilian bridge . . . gosh, we were just young lads back then.'

Gerhard declined, saying that he 'had better things to do that afternoon' and suggested that I too should seek out similar entertainment for myself. 'Perhaps you'll get lucky at the Isar beach!'

And I did get lucky that sunny afternoon, much as Gerhard had predicted, while also making a new friend in Heiner Hammer, who turned out to be an excellent swimmer. He was two years my senior and had fought in the war as a fighter pilot. A son of wealthy parents, he intended to study veterinary medicine. Just like me he'd known where the treacherous whirls underneath the Isar's Maximilian bridge were since childhood, and we just naturally kept an eye out to make sure bathers kept safe. On that day we actually saved a girl from drowning.

Just before taking our leave from each other that evening and seeing as we had discussed what each of us had in mind for our future, Heiner was very frank. 'Listen, Hans, I think somebody like you, seeing as you are far from stupid, should study for the *Abitur*.'*

During the following Sundays Heiner and I met up regularly at the riverbank. I had in fact signed up for evening courses, but by the end of August I admitted to Heiner that I simply couldn't cope with them any longer. I was much too exhausted to sit in class and study after a long day at work. 'Pity,' mused Heiner, 'I thought that somebody like you would definitely manage.'

As I was trying to explain myself a bit better we were actually sitting on a blanket just beside two bathing beauties, but disregarding them we both suddenly leapt to our feet, scarcely believing our eyes. A man was swimming really close to one of the most dangerous spots under the bridge where even good swimmers could get trapped by the weir 'The guy must be crazy!' screamed Heinz and I had to agree. 'He'll get sucked down!' Both of us jumped into the water but we could already see the man's head bobbing up and down and then he disappeared. We had a hell of a time pulling his heavy body away because of the current. Finally we heaved him to the surface and lugged him to shore. It had been in the nick of time. Spluttering and choking, he sat plonked on the grass, his coal-black eyes staring at

---

* The *Abitur* is Germany's principal high-school graduation certificate/university entrance qualification.

us in gratitude. Looking at his fat arms and legs and his rather large stomach bulging out of his blue swimming trunks, I couldn't help thinking that he certainly didn't look under-nourished.

Recovered and now breathing normally, the man thanked us profusely; Heiner was first to notice a tattoo on the inside of his arm, which might identify him as a previous inmate of a concentration camp.[*] It was only after the war that people such as Heiner and me learned about the atrocities the SS had committed in the camps and once again I could only thank my lucky stars that I had never been involved in any of these heinous acts as a soldier. Heinz felt similarly. 'Please, don't worry about us,' he mumbled when the man tried to apologise. 'Of course, we couldn't just sit there and watch you go under!'

'Thank you, thank you! Look here, just two months ago I moved into a villa in the Widenmayerstrasse. Please! Both of you! You absolutely must come and see me tomorrow evening. I wish to show my gratitude to the two of you – you have saved my life.'

Both of us knew the address. We rang the doorbell of a well-preserved and elegant villa built in the Jugendstil, seemingly untouched by any air raids, and the man we had saved the day before opened the door. We marvelled at his elegant appearance; he was dressed in a dapper light-grey suit with his dark wavy hair finely groomed, but his words disappointed. 'Oh, it's you . . . well, it's not exactly a good time,' he said in an off-hand way but then his tone warmed up. 'Just a moment, wait. I do have something for you two!'

He left the door slightly ajar, giving Heinz the opportunity to push it wider open with his foot. In front of us we could see how the entire wall to the right-hand side was stacked with different-sized boxes from top to bottom. Laughter and chatter emerged from some room; it was obvious that there was a gathering.

In the meantime, the man hastily ripped open one of the boxes, took something out, stepped back to the entrance and handed each of us a carton of American Chesterfield cigarettes. Not feeling in

---

[*] That the rescued man as a camp survivor seems highly implausible.
Perhaps his tattoo showed his blood group, indicating that he had been
an SS member, a status more consistent with his well-fed appearance.

the slightest uncomfortable about the fact that he wasn't giving us a minute more of his time, he said: 'Sorry, I cannot have you here. I've got important visitors. Many thanks and good luck!'

The door shut and the two of us just looked at each other perplexed, shrugging our shoulders. 'Hans,' muttered Heinz finally finding his tongue, 'it was hardly worth our while coming here. But, never mind!'

Both of us decided to put the incident behind us and agreed to meet up again the following week at our usual spot by the Isar. This time round it was me who got in trouble and it happened while playing badminton. I tripped barefoot into a hole in the ground and broke my foot in two spots. The doctor attending at the Kolping house decided that I needed to have the foot put in plaster and that I couldn't go to work. 'You really need to rest it, otherwise you might have a lasting injury!'

My employer was far from pleased when I told him and, as for me, I was even more disgruntled on hearing a week later that my lucrative position had been taken by an elderly man. I had counted on this being a secure job, and already had my eye on an affordable room in an old building in the Thierschplatz. This would give me some personal freedom, I had hoped, and allow me to remove myself from the stringent house rules of my current lodgings. In the meantime I had turned twenty.

It took me several months to find suitable alternative work. Germany, though, was recovering from the post-war chaos and the severe shortages of labour and materials, constant problems in food supply and reduced rations. The economy began to normalise and hunger was no longer a problem. When the currency reform was introduced in the summer of 1948 it, sadly for me, spelled the collapse of the black market in cigarettes.

When not filling in one application after another, I used every minute of my time to hunt for useful objects among the ruins of the buildings and so was able to store heaps of treasures in mother's rented *Schrebergarten*. This allotment was truly a godsend. You got to it via a water company building that hadn't been damaged, and since nearly all the employees there knew me as Frau Fackler's son I had no problem getting in at any time of day to stow away my bounty. I had a hunch that scrap was becoming a valuable commodity, particularly brass or copper parts, and before I knew it I had amassed a rather impressive stock which I had every intention of selling at a good profit. When a scrap-metal dealer offered me 800 DM and was even prepared to pick it all up with his van, I didn't hesitate. It was a lot of money and I had plans.

Luck was seemingly coming my way as when I bumped into Herr Eisler, an acquaintance of my mother's from before the war and a singer in the city's theatre choir. He recognised me immediately. 'Hans, still alive, good lad!' he shouted overjoyed, and asked me what I was up to. I told him about my job hunting but admitted that I hadn't been fortunate enough to find anything suitable so far. 'Would you be prepared to work in the theatre?' he wondered.

I didn't think twice. 'Brilliant ... something new.' Herr Eisler certainly didn't mess about and immediately asked that I come to the theatre the following day. 'Arrive at 1 o'clock, that's when rehearsals start. It so happens that the artistic director Johannes Lippl and his assistant Dörfler will be observing in the auditorium.' Before I could even start guessing how this could have anything to do with me, Herr Eisler explained that the creative team were seeking suitable candidates for extras and very small parts. 'I'm just thinking that they could well use somebody of your height – mind you, you won't get rich working for them.' I knew that much, of course. 'I'll be there!' I waved and we parted.

Until that day I had only known Johannes Lippl as the author of radio plays, such as *Der Passauer Wolf* or *Die Pfingstorgel*, but Herr Eisler had certainly made me very curious. The next day, there I was standing in front of the director and pulling myself up to my full height. Lippl eyed me up and down then casually remarked that I was the exact type he was looking for. 'Perfect height. We're starting work on *Egmont* on the day after tomorrow and you'll have the part of the soldier. Let's see what you make of it.'

Reporting the next morning to the Residenztheater I was told by the secretary that rehearsals would take place every day, starting at midday, and I would be paid DM 1.50 even if there was nothing for me to do. 'You'll be paid the same amount whether you're only an extra or are given a small part.' I didn't react much which the assistant noted with a smile. 'That's how it is these days, but many have started small with us and have become famous actors,' she said reassuringly and wished me good luck.

I'm not quite sure why, but leaving through the back entrance of the theatre building that first day left me feeling depressed. How would I manage on these meagre earnings, I worried, while trying to calculate my outgoings? But there I was, treading the boards. I played in *Egmont* for two days and then had a part in *Die Pfingstorgel* and thereafter in *Die Meistersinger von Nürnberg*.

I retain lovely memories from that time, especially of another quite unimpressive extra who swore that as soon as he 'had enough cash' he would attend drama school – he had always dreamed of a career in the theatre. He tried to convince me to follow suit. 'Hans,' he exclaimed knowingly, 'with your looks that should be a viable future for you!' But Helmut (I could never have guessed at the time that he would one day gain fame as 'Monaco Franze') wasn't able to turn an ex-joiner's apprentice into an actor.[*]

Joinery, however, didn't do it for me either any more as I simply couldn't see my future in this trade. Not having much luck with the employment office, I was hoping that doing some waitering might bump up my salary from being an extra. Fortunately a decently paid position at the (old) tearoom on the banks of the Kleinhesseloher See in the Englischer Garten opened up with the only issue being that one needed to be properly dressed for the job. Remembering the fabric from the defunct clothes factory which I had organised way back in Vacha and deposited with the mother of my erstwhile comrade, I decided to go and get it. Naturally, it wasn't the first time I had given thought to these pieces stored away there, but my deep-seated suspicion of the Russians had until then prevented me from travelling to the Soviet occupation zone.

---

[*] Hans's friend was presumably Helmut Fischer, who had a long career as a bit-part actor with limited success, before becoming famous in Germany as the title character in a TV detective series called *Monaco Franze* in the 1980s.

CHAPTER 12

Forced to Escape Again

It took me a while to find Heiner Rom's phone number in Geisa. Finally, at the end of December 1948, we managed to make contact and seeing as Heiner sounded remarkably cheerful as far as I could tell through the receiver, I became somewhat less fearful of the Russians.

'Gosh, Heiner, but of course we have all your stuff stored with us. Mother and I often mention you, as it happens,' his voice literally bubbled over. 'Absolutely, please come by and get your fabric . . . any time! Mother had even wanted to put the stuff in the wash at some point.'

I assured him that no cleaning of the fabric was necessary. 'It hasn't ever even been used, as you'll know. So, forget about bothering your mother with such nonsense!'

All while thanking him, I thought to myself that even had they sold the goods and kept the money for themselves seeing as they hadn't heard from me for such a long time, I wouldn't have taken it the wrong way. I told him as much. 'Never!' said Heiner incensed, 'we'd never do such a thing and we've never even entertained the thought.'

Happy, I promised Heiner I would visit them after New Year. 'I'd like to come at the beginning of January if that's all right!'

On 7 January I took the train to Fulda and from there a slow train to the last stop just before the border, I think it might have been called Schwarzbach, but don't remember exactly. But what I do remember, word for word, is what an older man told me during our journey, when we got chatting: 'Mark my words, young man, over there in the Ostzone, the Soviets are keeping a very sharp eye on West Germans like you. They tend not to be the friendliest . . . they are extremely suspicious ... I would not advise that you take the shortest and most direct route across, as that's where the checking is strictest. But there's a detour I can tell you about where they haven't set up all that many checkpoints.'

I followed his suggestion and late that same afternoon I took the route the man advised and which took me into 'the Zone' as it was referred to at the time. Long walks on foot were not an issue for me and I was therefore sure I could reach Geisa without having to use any further public transport.

Dusk was falling when two Russian soldiers ambled towards me, just when I was crossing into Geisa, close to Spahl. Too late to disappear behind the corner of a house, I simply sauntered along and walked past them with the most innocent expression I could muster. I managed to get ten metres ahead of them, but something about me must have rubbed them the wrong way: '*Stoi!*' they shouted – 'Stop!'

I turned and stood watching them stomping towards me with their high-booted legs and one of them stretching out his hand with the gesture by then well-known to me. I handed him my identification card while the other guy fumbled around with the strap of his brand-new Kalashnikov. Turning to his colleague, the older of the two said something in Russian to him, all the while clenching my ID card in his hand. 'Coming with!' he then grunted in bad German. 'To mayor in village.'

The two soldiers seemed familiar with the place. Walking ahead of them, some one hundred metres across the village, I noticed curtains being drawn or twitching furtively in the houses we passed, but the streets themselves were totally empty. I got the distinct feeling that the inhabitants wished to have very little to do with the Russians.

The mayor lived in a small one-family house with a few stone steps leading up to its entrance. I entered at gunpoint. Led to the kitchen I could see the mayor, a man greying at the temples and with snow-white moustache, seated on a black leather couch. The only other person in the room was a young girl who I assumed was his daughter. Sitting at the kitchen table, she gripped a large German shepherd dog firmly by its neck while it growled menacingly from underneath. 'Lux, naughty boy! All is good, now sit!' Belying his appearance, the dog cowered fearfully and returned to his blanket.

My coat was a bit of a patchwork, made up of pieces of remnant army fabric – not an unusual look at the time, yet it didn't go over too well with the occupiers. Standing in the middle of the kitchen, I was ordered by the younger of the two Russians to take it off immediately. Left with no other choice than to obey the order of *'Ausziehen!'* I had just about managed to put it over the back of a chair when the other soldier grabbed hold of my leather pouch which I tended to carry slung over my chest. Ripping it off me, he unzipped it and out flew two pictures of myself in the RAD wearing uniform. I had brought them along to show them to Heiner but cursed myself for having been so careless.

Turning the bag inside out the Russian triumphantly pointed to my cash, my discharge certificate, a picture of my mother, my return ticket and some other stuff while declaring at the top of his voice that I was surely an enemy of the Russians. 'You being spy!' he shouted. 'No!' I shouted back. 'I only want to visit an old friend – nothing else!'

He replied he didn't believe me, while I insisted I was speaking the truth. 'What else would I be doing here?' I asked, quite incensed.

'We soon be know!' he said sternly, looking at the mayor who had been observing the entire scene without uttering a word. 'You,' he addressed the mayor with the familiar *Du*, very pointedly not according him the respectful *Sie*-form befitting his rank. 'You, going with us in your room. I want speaking to you and make telephone call!'

The three left the kitchen for a small neighbouring room, leaving the door behind them wide open. It wasn't hard for me to see that the two Russians, their backs turned to me, were standing in front of the phone, but for how long, I wondered? 'Might I use the toilet?' I asked the girl, who threw me an anxious look but she sympathised. 'First door on your right, next to the entrance.'

Calmly I walked to the entrance, opened it with one swift movement, jumped into the front garden, hopped over the low fence and ran as fast as I could down the road away from the mayor's house, breathlessly reaching the edge of the forest. There, I ducked into a hollow in the ground offering me a tiny bit of protection. Russian shouting erupted behind me and I could make out the word '*stoi!*' called out several times. Seconds later the din of gunshots echoed through the landscape – the Russians must have emptied their entire magazines – and resounded through the night of this peaceful and sleepy village.

My pursuers must have suspected me to be somewhere behind the mayor's house, as when it all seemed to have calmed down I cautiously lifted my head and in the dim light of the lamp hanging above the door caught sight of two dark figures disappearing to the back.

Let me get away from here as fast as possible, I thought, and followed a well-trodden snow path into the wood. Should the mayor be forced to search for me, I'd surely be sniffed out by the dog, and that would be the end of me.

It was pitch-black around me but it served me well as the light of the moon could easily have given me away. But while the dense forest kept me well protected, I couldn't see where I was heading and lost all sense of direction. Groping for one tree trunk after another I was only making wild guesses as to where the border might be. The cold crept through my clothing and once again I cursed my sheer stupidity in having packed those pictures. Where would they deport me to if they picked me up again? The more anxious I became, desperately forging my way through the snow, the more lost I felt.

Fear of being transported away, to God knows which part of Russia, kept me marching on, through the night, clutching bushes, blindly feeling trunks or flailing my hands into empty space – the forest seemed endless. Many hours seemed to have gone by when at long last I saw a faint glimmer of light ahead of me. I am approaching the West, I sighed with relief and hastened my pace, only to realise a few minutes later that I must have walked in a circle: I stood at the boundary of Spahl which I had escaped just hours before. The village lay right there in the dark. All was quiet and seemingly peaceful. Only one building was lit, a restaurant it looked like, and there seemed to be some life there.

Tentatively sneaking closer, I could hear dull voices belonging to a few men. Fervently I hoped that there were no Russians among them, but I couldn't hear any Russian spoken. Cautiously I first opened the door to the corridor and then the one to the dining room. I had barely set foot in the room when one of the men leapt to his feet and hurriedly asked: 'Are you the one who escaped the Russians this morning?'

'Yes,' I responded calmly and, equally composed, added that I wasn't a spy as suspected by the Russians.

'That's obvious, of course, we all know that – but actually none of us really care. Is there any way that we can be of help to you?'

What a relief – not only were they not prepared to give me away to the occupiers, they were also keen to help. I felt quite emotional. But conscious of how precarious my situation was, I simply asked them whether they could possibly help me retrieve my coat and bag which were, I gathered, still at the mayor's house. 'If you would be good enough to take me to the house, then I won't have to go looking for it in the night.'

Several of the guests immediately got up and asked if they could escort me personally to the mayor's home, but the landlord fortunately butted in. 'Stop making a fuss! Hannes will be plenty.'

Hannes was about my age, took my arm and walked me out into the dark road. He already knew my name. Turning his face right and left, he whispered that he knew where Birgit's bedroom was located. 'If we take care to wake her gently, the dog will keep quiet and nobody'll notice anything.'

'Is Birgit the mayor's daughter?'

'Indeed, but she is okay, and her father as well.'

A few minutes later, walking to the back of the mayor's house, Hannes softly knocked on a window in the garden. It opened just enough for us to hear Birgit's voice: 'Who's there?' she asked softly.

Hannes identified himself – they obviously knew each other. 'I've brought somebody along,' explained Hannes, 'and we can't have Lux making any noise, please.' Birgit told him that the dog was sleeping in the kitchen and wouldn't hear anything if we kept the noise to a minimum.

The window was now fully ajar and I could see the girl's light nightgown shimmering in the dark. 'Who do you have with you, Hannes?' she enquired, still whispering.

Hannes briefly told her, but I butted in. 'Can you get me my coat and bag back?'

'Unfortunately, not,' answered Birgit, in a slightly louder tone. 'The Russians have taken your bag, but yes, your coat, your cap and your scarf are still here. Mind you, the men said they would pick them up tomorrow morning. They were hopping mad you'd slipped out of their hands,' she reported, adding in the same breath that neither she nor her father wanted to mess with the Russians.

'But surely you can't let me go without my winter coat!' I pleaded. 'It's freezing cold out here and I have no clue how I'll even manage to get back to Munich without any money. And . . . my return ticket was also in that leather bag.'

Hannes, who probably like me had been a soldier in the war, felt it was now his turn to get things back on track. 'Birgit,' he spoke forcefully. 'Cut it out, for God's sake. You can simply tell those Russians that during the night there was a burglary at your house. Must have been professionals, you'll say, as they were silent as a mouse and your Lux didn't even bark once.' Hannes had it figured out. 'And now, as soon as Hans has all his belongings, I'll take him to the border. It's not all that far.'

Birgit seemed to give it some thought, as for a few seconds we didn't hear a peep out of her. 'Fine,' she whispered, 'but first I absolutely must tell father. Wait a moment.' A few minutes later Birgit handed me my coat, cap and scarf out of the window. 'Father knows,' she told us quietly, 'and he agrees with what you've come up with. But get away from here as soon and as fast as you can.'

'Thank you,' I couldn't help speaking in a normal voice only to be hushed by Hannes.

Relieved, I was just about to slip on my coat but was immediately rushed by Hannes. 'Hans, come on, I'll feel a lot better when you've crossed that damned border. The Russians are not to be trusted.'

A tollgate erected across a narrow dirt road marked the end of the Ostzone. Hannes must have known that the Russians occasionally kept watch over this part of the countryside as, shortly before reaching the barrier, he grabbed my arm and stood still, listening out in the night for any untoward noises. It was January 1949 and the borders had not yet been tightly secured as unfortunately would be the case later on.

When we couldn't hear a sound, Hannes suddenly started speaking in a normal tone advising me how to get to the police station. 'You haven't committed a crime,' he began, 'so surely they'll help.' Stretching out his hand he wished me good luck. 'Have a safe return trip to Munich.'

I shook his hand long and firmly, thanking him for his excellent scheme to make up the story about the burglary, for getting my coat back and for accompanying me. I had no difficulty finding the police station but the two sleepy officers didn't seem in the least bit interested in me. In fact, I sensed that one of them was particularly annoyed about my unlikely story. 'D'you really think that we'll issue you with a document which'll get you on a train back to Munich?' he blustered. 'You can forget about that right now. But, tell you what. Get yourself home, go to the local police station and,' his tone now friendlier, 'they'll issue you with a fresh ID. We cannot help you any further here.'

Just before dawn broke I was already sat waiting on one of the benches at the train station, my eyes peeled for the first morning train to pull in, while mulling over how I would explain my situation to the ticket inspector. Then my eyes fell on a pretty young girl sauntering onto the platform. Wearing a tight light-grey skiing outfit and carrying her skis across her shoulders, she approached me. When she was just about to pass by the bench, I couldn't help myself and tried striking up a conversation. 'Hi there! You're certainly up and about early!' Not in the least bit surprised, she smilingly told me that she was off to the Garmisch ski resort.

She seemed a very chatty and open sort of young woman who immediately launched into telling me all about herself. Her father, an obviously well-to-do porcelain shop owner in Selb for whom she was working, had only allowed her to take a break once she had taken care of some pressing matters. 'My brother is already there.

He took my luggage in his VW. Beetle and went ahead of me . . . But what's up with you? Why the long face?'

I was heartened by the fact that this young person, apparently with wealthy parents and of a jolly nature, was giving me space to recount how I had got myself into this tight spot.

Introducing ourselves to each other, she didn't hesitate to offer a solution. 'Herr Fackler, look, this isn't a problem at all. Take this,' she declared, matter-of-factly pulling a purse from her zipped pocket and stretching out a few bills. 'Go and buy yourself a ticket. You can pay me back and send me the money to Garmisch. I'll give you my address once we're on the train. But hurry!' she pointed to the train that meanwhile had pulled in, 'It'll be departing soon.'

We were using the *Du*-form even before we changed over to the train that took us directly to Munich from where Ingrid would continue to Garmisch. While we were walking along the Munich platform it didn't take much for her to agree that she would accompany me back to my room where I would be able to return her money. 'Sure, Hans,' she laughed, 'but let me just call my brother and let him know I'll only be arriving tomorrow.'

'Not a problem at all,' I responded yet had to worry out loud that my landlady would not allow any female company. 'So, we'll just have to be mighty quiet when we get there,' she giggled. 'Ah, that's fun! Makes our secret date even more exciting!'

The following day, when I took her to the train station, she confessed that she was due to get married in four weeks. 'Hans, don't get me wrong, we had a good time. But my father has picked a wealthy heir to a factory for me to marry . . . someone who'll be able to offer me a good life. Angry?'

'No, Ingrid. I can't offer you a factory but what I can do is wish you the best of luck and a wonderful holiday.' I would be lying, though, if I said that this farewell didn't profoundly depress me.

Some three weeks later I was once more the owner of a valid ID card. A tailor I knew suggested a decent price to provide me with made-to-measure suits from the fabric I had already mentioned but which still lay in storage at the home of Hannes and his mother. The tailor, one of those self-assured types, guaranteed that in the suits he would tailor for me I would look better than my boss. 'So, what are you waiting for. Let's have that fabric already!'

This time round, together with three other lads from Thuringia I crossed the border, choosing a well-concealed path through the woods. Baffled at how easy this particular crossing was, I once again chastised myself for not having taken more precautions the time before.

The reunion with Hannes and his mother moved me to the core as for several days we revisited memories from our time together at the army hospital.

Two days later, I delivered the fabric to Oskar my tailor. He inspected the material with a few expert hand movements and thought that the amount definitely allowed for two suits. 'Quite surprising really, how fabulous the quality was even up to the very end of the war,' he remarked, wondering out loud for whom the material might have been intended. 'But, seeing that I am doing all the work, I'll keep whatever's left on the roll for myself, it'll be my payment.'

CHAPTER 13

Securing my Future – After Some False Starts

My work as a waiter plus being doled out the odd small part at the theatre didn't fulfil me in the long run. Scouring the papers for job ads, I read one which sounded suitable. A company in La Chaux de Fonds in Neuchâtel, a canton in Switzerland famous for watch-making, was looking for workers who could handle tools and precision instruments to cut gold and other precious metals into tiny parts. The starting salary was 800 Francs and would increase with time. Lodging was available in town. And to top it all off I would, I thought, get to travel and live in Switzerland. It seemed like an amazing opportunity and certainly a better option than hanging around in Germany. My application proved successful.

That autumn – it was now October 1949 – I took the train to La Chaux de Fonds and the reception from the company manager was friendly enough though candid. 'Herr Fackler,' he launched into his welcome, 'so far I've only had the best experiences with German workers and I can only hope that you won't disappoint. Your predecessor sadly fell to his death while mountain-climbing around the Jura. Are you a climber too?'

'No,' I replied, 'what with my war injury to my leg, I couldn't scale your mountains even if I wanted to. But,' I hastily assured him, 'I will do my utmost to fulfil my duties at work, I have no problem standing or walking.'

Perhaps I should not have been so forthcoming. Eyeing me for a while, the manager then carefully asked his question: 'You were a soldier, then?' I nodded in silence and to my relief he no longer seemed interested or certainly didn't want to dwell on it. 'Well,

Herr Fackler, once you've been trained and are familiar with our manufacturing process, I can promise that you'll be making more money. Let me explain your duties: You'll be looking after the machinery in what we call Hall 3. Our calculations have revealed that for optimal production the machines must not remain idle for more than absolutely necessary. We export our products around the globe, competition is huge and it's getting tougher by the day. I ask you not to disappoint us.'

Right from the very start I felt comfortable both in the town and at my workplace. It was eye-opening to experience a country which had been able to live in peace – and for the Swiss the terms war and its consequences were alien. I was startled at the difference between this and my own country, where the wounds of the war were still raw and painful. While this senseless struggle among nations had ruined our homeland, here, in Switzerland the world seemed intact and I felt safe.

Seeing as I had no family nor any social obligations, I would often find myself the last one to leave but the first to arrive at work the next morning, ensuring that I could get my machine up and running as early as possible. Would you believe it, but after only three months, much to my delight, I was making 1,000 francs? Converting the francs into Deutschmarks I considered myself as rich as Croesus.

A year later and totally unexpectedly, however, the owner of the company informed his employees that the firm was obliged to file for bankruptcy – all due, he explained, to the immense pressures of competition from foreign countries; I believe he mentioned Sweden and China.

The head of personnel of another firm must have somehow got wind that I was a very capable and reliable employee, and offered me a job right then and there. The firm produced fine watch springs which would then be fitted into top quality timepieces, but this particular owner was the stingy sort and the salary he suggested did not reflect the experience I had accumulated by then.

This, however, wasn't the only reason that I decided to return to Germany. I longed to return to my homeland, so applied to a company in Pforzheim which produced small and ultra-small watch screws and was searching for someone with a skill that by now was on my CV. When I actually received the offer, the Swiss boss suddenly turned extremely generous. 'But Herr Fackler, listen, as of today you'll be making 1,100 Francs here in my business! That's not an amount to sneeze at! I urge you, dear Herr Fackler, think carefully about moving away!'

I thanked Herr Knüsachli but declined. 'It's too late for that, I'm afraid.'

Refusing his offer undeniably gave me some inner satisfaction, but as it turned out I didn't strike it lucky with the firms I was picking – only six months into my job the Pforzheim outfit also couldn't escape bankruptcy. This was somewhat upsetting but in truth I was longing to return to Munich, my home town, where this time I found a job at the big MAN engineering firm.

Even during my training period at MAN I made a decent income and in 1955 was promoted to being in charge of quality control in the department of high-precision parts. Despite the good salary, I couldn't resist accepting an offer by Anker Werke, a company in Bielefeld who appointed me as the Munich salesman for their products. Both the remuneration and the job description were too tempting. Deep down I felt that convincing others to acquire a machine which I myself believed in was right up my alley. The cash registers manufactured by Anker were of solid German work-manship and I was proud of their quality. My brief training period in Bielefeld proved challenging and had its pitfalls, but it was plain sailing thereafter alongside a salary as a district sales manager which was higher than anything I had ever earned previously.

After a particularly profitable day in Freising north of Munich, an area I'd been assigned to cover by Anker, I felt I was due for a bit of a rest. What then unfolded would remain ingrained in my memory. Sitting comfortably and happy with both myself and the world at the Café Eggerdinger, while watching passers-by through the front window, a man, getting off his bike and then entering the café, caught my attention. There was a haughty look about him when he approached my table and, seeing as I was sitting by myself with a free chair across from me, he pulled it back and plonked himself down while asking in a thick Bavarian accent and somewhat cursory manner whether I permitted him to do so. As I was in a chatty mood in any event, I replied that of course he could join me and, attempting a bit of humour, added that the table didn't belong to me. Nonchalantly lighting a cigarette, he gazed at me across the glimmering flame and said that he hadn't seen me before. Had I just moved into the area?

'No, I've spent the day selling cash registers to a few shops around here – they are great machines which save employees time recording the daily takings as our Anker devices perform this task automatically.' I was the perfect sales representative. The man sounded intrigued. 'Are there many types of such cash registers?' He then listened to me attentively as I explained the various different machines we had on the market and for which particular purpose each one was appropriate. Our conversation covered all kinds of topics and I marvelled at how well-informed this man was despite giving the outward impression of being quite average. Suddenly he seemed to be in a great hurry as he waved the waitress to our table and asked for the bill in his strong Bavarian accent. He got up and was about to leave when he turned to me once more and quite loudly said that if Anker didn't come up with a cleverer machine than they were offering I should build one myself.

Laughing, the waitress told me that this man was well-known in the area – he was the entertainer called Roider Jackl.* His sharp tongue, she continued, was generally not kindly received by the rich and powerful as he had no qualms about touching raw nerves and insulting those higher up. Apparently, she maintained, he hadn't even shied away from criticising Nazi big-wigs. Then it dawned on me that of course I knew him from radio shows I listened to quite frequently.

The gap in the market for cash registers was filled faster than I expected and I swiftly moved to the car dealer Niedermeier & Reich, but not for long. Though I had grown fond of travelling by car in

---

* Roider Jackl was an entertainer who performed in the Bavarian dialect, specialising in somewhat rude rhyming songs.

my role as sales representative, when it actually came to selling cars I realised how very unsuitable I was. My luck held out as the Bavarian Insurance Company located at Karolinenplatz 5 offered me a position as an insurance account manager entailing a salary well above average.

By nature a sociable fellow, I was able to build a clientele within a relatively short period of time during which I gained respect among the firm's management and within the sector as a whole, yet the work also allowed for time to pursue hobbies I had previously only heard about. My winter holidays were spent in Kitzbühel, I took the hunters' exam and enjoyed going on hunting trips with clients or friends.

My then girlfriend Gabriele Heirich was a lawyer as was her father who owned the hunting grounds around Zellmühleck where years before I had spent time with the RAD, and now, here I was again, this time to indulge in the hunting sport.

Among those sitting for the hunter exam was a Herr Seiler who was employed in a legal office. Around springtime of 1967 he asked whether I would take his cousin on my holiday to Kitzbühel. 'Hans,' he confided in me, 'you'd do me and the young lady a great favour. She is an assistant in a pharmacy and does nothing but work. She must get out of there and have some fun!'

Happy to be helpful and not in the least bothered by his request, I immediately agreed. 'If that's all, then sure! The day after tomorrow I'd like to get away for a bit and Kitzbühel will do me nicely. Where should I pick up the young lady?'

Herr Seiler said he'd call her immediately so that she would have no time to give his idea much thought and simply do as she was told. He gave me her address and phone number while letting me know that the young woman was thirteen years my junior and very pretty. Never would I have dreamt that she would one day become my wife and mother of my two children, Steffi and Florian. But that's what happened and that same year I was able to build a house in Glonn, a market community in the county of Ebersberg where I still live.*

---

* Hans Fackler passed away in July 2019.

Unfortunately, my wife and I later parted ways but my children and I remain close.

Meanwhile my mother lived in an apartment in Munich where she was happy and pleased with her life until she passed away at the age of eighty. It took me quite a while to get over this loss but life had to continue, I told myself, and I resolved to enjoy everything that was coming my way.

Let me not forget to relay an anecdote dating back to 1962 which happened well before my marriage. Although I spent most of my free time with my then fiancée, I was reluctant to give up getting together with friends for an evening out, mostly at the Hahnhof in the Leopoldstrasse.

That particular evening my mates and I were gathered around a table having a terrific time as always. We may have been slightly tipsy but certainly weren't drunk. Each of us had parked somewhere in the neighbourhood, except for Dinser who had arrived on foot as he owned a shop close by and didn't have far to walk. Calling it a night after some three hours at the restaurant, all of us felt perfectly confident about getting behind the wheel as we knew that we hadn't gone over the drink-drive limit.

On leaving the Hahnhof, however, we had a nasty surprise. Against our will we were pulled into a crowd of demonstrating youths who soon got into a tumultuous fistfight with the police. Some officers grabbed hold of me, thinking I was one of the rioters, dragged me to their police van parked right in front of the Siegestor, shoved me to the doors and despite vigorous protestations on my part forced me into the rear cabin. I'm not sure why, but I was really outraged while the guys around me took it in their stride. Perhaps I had simply had enough of men in uniforms. In the end, we simply had to bow to the authorities.

Looking down at the pushing and shoving on Leopoldstrasse which was gradually petering out, I thought I recognised a young man who was talking to two officers only a few metres away from our police van. It was a Herr Schreiber, who about a year previously had worked in my office in the Bayerische Versicherungskammer as a legal clerk to gain experience in the insurance sector.

I had heard somewhere that he had been offered a senior position with the police. Suddenly, perhaps he could feel me staring at him, he looked up and also recognised me. 'Herr Fackler!' he said with some surprise, 'So you also belong with these hooligans?'

'Certainly not, Herr Schreiber!' I quickly replied. 'Let me assure you that me and my colleagues were on a night out at the Hahnhof – surely you know it, as perhaps you'll recall that both of us were there together quite often!' I wanted to impress my innocence and thought that it wouldn't hurt to name-drop. 'We've got nothing to do with those hooligans. And they've even arrested Dr Kulmann – surely you remember him!'

'Of course I do,' he reassured me and turning to his two officers he must have clarified matters as shortly thereafter I was permitted to get down from the van. 'Thank you kindly, Herr Schreiber, and please spare a moment for our lawyer, Dr Kulmann!'

Herr Schreiber couldn't have been more gracious. 'Most certainly, most certainly, we'll sort this all out. Make sure you get home safely!'

Much to my embarrassment the moment when I was arrested had been caught on camera and the following day my colleagues had a feast, drooling over a picture in the *Neue Illustrierte*. It was unpleasant having to fend off the insults branding me as a rowdy thug who had mixed with the 'Schwabinger Krawalle'.

The sixties were not only marked by student unrest and rioting, however. For many people of my generation these years actually resembled a Golden Age. The so-called *Deutsches Wirtschafts-wunder*, the miraculous recovery of our economy, signalled rapid growth for practically all industries and infused our society with swathes of optimism. Was it an act of justice towards us young men who had participated in the war and suffered and bled on all fronts? Germany's revival certainly benefited youngish people like me, as the enormous number of lives lost meant that there was a labour shortage and workers were in high demand.

The Cold War, beginning soon after the war, shaped the ensuing conflict between the communist bloc and the West during the second half of the twentieth century and prevented the victorious nations from committing the same mistakes as they had after World

War I. Most fortunately, therefore, it didn't allow them to shame us, the defeated, in a manner that would once again sow the seeds for new conflicts. Instead, provisions for peace were delayed indefinitely while the respective occupied zones were integrated into each side's own political system, especially in the three western zones, turning out to be much to the advantage of a young new Germany which by then had evolved from erstwhile enemy to crucial and close ally of the Western powers.

Because German industry almost totally lay in ruins, the country rallied to revive it with the help of state-of-the art machinery and thus gained the edge over its competitors.

Against the backdrop of the chaos and misery characterising the early post-war years, many compatriots who belonged to my generation were able to flourish in careers for which they may not necessarily have been prepared – and I was one of them. My steady and comfortable income allowed me to put behind me the uncertainties and troubles that had plagued me during the earlier post-war years. Though trained as a joiner, it was, in the end, the insurance business which enabled me to build up my life and enjoy my wealth and the social circles I mixed in. The hunting association, in my mind, stands out as a particularly enriching pastime as it allowed me to form many solid male friendships and, with a nod to my charming daughter-in-law, I also became a respected personality in high society. Two wonderful grandchildren, both boys, come to visit their grandpa often.

From my comrades at the front I would hear nothing, but continued my friendship with Franz, with whom I had escaped the Russians and hiked through Thuringia. Just after we had completed the construction of our house, he visited me, sadly just that once. The younger of two sons of a farmer in Pocking located in Lower Bavaria, he could no longer see a future for himself in his home town and had moved to Cologne with his then girlfriend, eventually his wife. While we men had a jolly old time chatting away into the night about shared memories and enjoying a wholesome platter of Bavarian cold cuts his wife was rather cold, examining us and our home with judging eyes.

Fortune generally was kind to us survivors of the Second World War, but we cannot rid ourselves of the horrors we had to live through and the guilt for what we became entangled in against our will and through no fault of our own. I was to remain profoundly affected by my experiences as a young soldier. The dreadful scenes of the sinking *Wilhelm Gustloff* were forever to remain engraved in my mind. To this day I still hear the cries in my sleep: the screams of the drowning.

War, as we soldiers knew first-hand, is the absolute worst scourge of mankind, impacting not just on our lot, but above all on innocent civilians, women, men and children. It therefore falls on us that those responsible in government and tasked with looking after the younger generation safeguard peace for our grandchildren and, if possible, beyond. There is no duty more important!